# GreatChefs®
## OF HAWAI'I

Licensed to Mutual Publishing by
Great Chefs® Television/Publishing
747 Magazine Street
New Orleans, LA 70130
1-800-321-1499

ISBN 1-56647-595-3
Library of Congress Catalog Card
Number: 2003100944

Design by Sistenda Yim

First Printing, May 2003

www.greatchefs.com



Mutual Publishing
1215 Center Street, Suite 210
Honolulu, Hawai'i 96816
Telephone (808) 732-1709
Fax (808) 734-4094
e-mail: mutual@lava.net
www.mutualpublishing.com



Printed in Korea

# Great Chefs® OF HAWAI'I

## By Kaui Philpotts

MUTUAL PUBLISHING

# TABLE OF CONTENTS

❖ ❖ ❖

❖ ❖ ❖

## Desserts

❖ ❖ ❖

❖ ❖ ❖

❖ ❖ ❖

# FOREWORD

When I began writing about food in Hawai'i 20 years ago, I had no idea I'd been assigned to cover the hottest breaking story in the Islands.

I'd booked a front-row table just in time for the revolution. A generation ago there was good food in the Islands, but you had to look to find it. It could be found in little ethnic restaurants with unpronounceable names and Formica™-topped tables. Or at lunch wagons that sold a cross-cultural mix of entrées on paper plates. Or at private parties and lū'aus where the buffet table might offer Hawaiian kālua pig and lomilomi salmon, Chinese duck and noodles with char siu, Japanese teriyaki, tonkatsu and sushi, Vietnamese spring rolls, Filipino lumpia, Korean kalbi and kim chee, Thai curry and green papaya salad.

This was not fashionable food. It was just food we liked, and shared among ourselves. It certainly wasn't the food we ordered in white-tablecloth restaurants. And it was definitely not the food we served to visitors.

We served visitors what we thought they liked—French onion soup, Caesar salad, chateaubriand, duck à l'orange, chocolate mousse. Surrounded by an ocean teeming with fish, we flew in frozen sole and served sole almandine. We even served visitors food they thought was Hawaiian, but wasn't. We covered chicken with sliced pineapple, sprinkled macadamia nuts on imported fish.

But then, at first slowly, things began to change.

From France, from the Mainland, from Japan, the new resorts brought in highly creative young chefs. Hawai'i began to develop more homegrown talent—chefs with Hawaiian or Asian or mixed backgrounds who went to school, absorbed the craft, and had the advantage of knowing the territory. It occurred to these young chefs that they would never become truly great unless they exploited the fresh ingredients around them.

And what ingredients they found. The ocean teemed with some of the best seafood in the world—'ahi, mahimahi, opah, 'opakapaka, shutome. An infant aquaculture industry provided freshwater prawns and cold-water lobster.

Warm and sunny, Hawai'i could grow virtually anything, not just sugar and pineapple. The chefs began talking to the farmers. You began to hear about fresh herbs on Moloka'i. Chocolate on the Big Island. Strawberries, onions, and blue potatoes on the slopes of Upcountry Maui. Baby lettuces, watercress, and lemongrass just a 20-minute drive from downtown Honolulu. The alliance between chefs and farmers created a rapidly evolving regional cuisine. Hawai'i was America's only tropical state. It burst forth with flavors no other part of the country could provide.

And Hawai'i had one other crucial ingredient—a resident population already accustomed to mixing and matching a multitude of Polynesian, Eastern, and Western flavors. It was an audience who responded enthusiastically when a few daring chefs began charring 'ahi with Japanese spices and serving it with a lilikoi sauce. Or filling a taro basket with Peking duck and wild mushrooms. Or steaming local fish in a combination of Provençal herbs and Hawaiian-style seaweeds.

All the tastes we had cultivated all those years in secret were out of the closet. Better yet, they were on the restaurant table—done with the precision and power of skilled chefs.

Hawai'i went food crazy. New restaurants sprang up. Menus changed daily. Going out for dinner grew into an adventure. Dozens of chefs, emboldened, cooked up their own versions of Hawaiian regional cuisine. Their contributions were hotly debated, analyzed, and enjoyed. Overnight small farmers became celebrities, the cutting edge of agriculture. And everyone who took pleasure in great food profited—including visitors to the Islands, who turned out not to have wanted sole almandine after all.

Great Chefs® has done a tremendous job, first of finding this culinary revolution in the middle of the Pacific, and then of documenting it so beautifully. And I have to salute my friend Kaui Philpotts, who fifteen or so years ago first introduced me to the blue potatoes and 'Ulupalakua strawberries of Upcountry Maui. It's no surprise to anyone who knows her that Kaui has written such a useful and enjoyable book.

Even reading the lists of ingredients, the names of the dishes, you can feel the warm sun, hear the tradewinds rustling through the palm fronds, and almost taste paradise.

Aloha. Enjoy.
John Heckathorn, Editor
*Honolulu Magazine*

# HAWAIIAN FOOD

From Native Culture to the New Cuisine

Think Hawaiian food, and you may conjure up a dish with a sticky-sweet pineapple sauce worthy of a fifties cookbook. Or even worse, you may recall a tale of culinary horror from a neighbor who attended a lūʻau for tourists at a Waikīkī resort hotel. But there's a lot more to Hawaiian food than these sad examples. A revolution that is nothing short of phenomenal has occurred in island cuisine in the past decade, led by young chefs working with fresh foods from Asia, Hawaiʻi, and California.

The first Hawaiians were Polynesians who arrived in two groups, the first from the Marquesas somewhere around 300 A.D. and another from Tahiti around 900 A.D. In their seaworthy voyaging canoes they brought all their staples: kalo (taro root), rock salt, ʻulu (breadfruit), ʻuala (sweet potato), puaʻa (pigs), moa (chicken), ʻīlio (dogs), kukui (candlenut tree), coconuts, and bananas.

The water was sweet in these isolated islands in the middle of the Pacific. Fish were abundant in the sea, as were limu (seaweed) and ʻopihi (shellfish) close to shore. To their diet the Hawaiians added the hōʻiʻo fern, the spinachlike leaves of the taro root (lūʻau) and the taro's crimson stalks (hāhā). As the society and culture developed, the men became the preparers of food, building fire pits lined with hot volcanic rock called imu, while the women made the family's clothing from kapa cloth (the pounded bark of the wauke, or mulberry tree). Religious significance was placed on certain foods, such as bananas, coconuts, pork, and shark's meat, and women were forbidden to eat them, on the threat of death. Men and women dined separately, and many other strict rules of conduct directed their lives. It was not until 1819, when the great Queen Kaʻahumanu, regent and widow of Kamehameha I, sat down with her badly shaken young son and heir Liholiho and ate a meal with

him in public, that the old kapu (tabu) against men and women eating at the same table was thrown out.

In March 1820, Hawaiian spiritual life underwent a radical change with the arrival of the first Protestant missionaries from New England aboard the *Thaddeus*. In the years between the "discovery" by Captain James Cook in 1778 of what he called the Sandwich Islands and the arrival of the missionaries, Hawaiians had been introduced to hard tack, salt-cured salmon, and beef from ships headed for China to trade furs from the American Northwest. These merchant sailors also brought with them liquor and a bawdy lifestyle.

The New England missionaries and other early merchant settlers from England, Scotland, France, and Germany combined the imported foods of their homelands with what was fresh and available locally. Many of the earliest adventurers married Hawaiian women and stayed in the islands, further blending dietary habits.

By the middle of the nineteenth century, a need for cheap field labor developed due to the planting of sugar cane and pineapple. The native Hawaiian population had declined in alarming numbers because of disease and dissipation, and the Hawaiian temperament, while hardworking and good-natured, was not suited to the grueling labor patterns imposed by the plantation owners.

Waves of immigrants came from Asia, first from China, then from Japan, Korea, and the Philippines. Later in the century, workers were imported from the Portuguese islands of Madeira and the Azores, as well as Puerto Rico. With them came their cuisines.

Plantation families imported what they could from back home, and adapted traditional recipes to what was available or could be grown in Hawai'i. Every plantation home had a small vegetable garden, and on weekends families went to the ocean to gather limu (seaweed), 'opihi (limpets), and fish from the shore. Net and shore fishing was popular.

All plantation camps had shady mango trees, small lime trees, and aloe cactus for burns and rashes. The Chinese planted lychee trees and juicy sweet star fruit (carambola). The Japanese made sure they had turnips (daikon)

for their pickles. The Koreans planted cabbage and small red chilies for their kim chee. From the Portuguese came backyard stone ovens for bread making, and fragrant vegetable and bean soups as well as pungent vinegar-laced roasts called vinha d'alhos.

By the 1930s, a robust folk cuisine had been well established throughout the island chain. All the different nationalities, as they began intermarrying, reveled in each other's festivals and food.

Restaurants and hotels, however, ignored "local food" and served dishes that reflected the tastes of the mainland United States and Europe. At great expense, foods like fresh strawberries, beef, and lamb were flown in to be served in the best dining rooms at luxury resorts. Local food was considered too ethnic, unsophisticated, and definitely inferior.

But then things changed. Influenced by the new American cuisine movement on the mainland, the younger chefs who came to oversee the kitchens of the new resorts that popped up in the late seventies and through the eighties became interested in local ingredients. Hawaiian Regional Cuisine was nurtured by a group of seminal chefs who developed local contacts among farmers and fishermen and showcased local ingredients. The ripples of that movement spread rapidly.

The result was the kind of food featured in this book: fresh island ingredients and dishes combined with the foods and cuisines of the many cultures that have become part of today's Hawai'i.

In this book we have featured recipes from Hawai'i's finest restaurant and resort chefs who appear on the Great Chefs® of Hawai'i television series. All the recipes have been revised and tested for the home cook, and we have provided a glossary of ingredients and Hawaiian food terms indicating substitutions whenever possible. We urge you to prepare these dishes for your family and friends. We know you will be surprised and delighted. Some recipes are complicated and geared toward cooks with advanced skills, but most are well within the abilities of the home cook.

Native Hawaiians have an expression—Hele mai a'i—that means "Come here and eat." This greeting was traditionally extended easily and often to friends, family, and even total strangers passing by.

We hope you will use this book, then call your friends and neighbors and say, "Hele mai a'i."

# Appetizers

■ ■ ■

There is no better way to sample the complex flavors of Hawaiian cuisine than to graze through the appetizer courses on any island restaurant menu. The same goes for using this book. Chefs are often at their most creative in developing appetizers. Here you will find Asian sauces and dressings with miso and chilis, and smoked and seared fish with fresh fruit salsas.

# 'Ahi Cake

Serves 8

A Hawaiian version of a terrine, this 'ahi cake combines the color and flavor of sweet Maui onion, eggplant, and seared 'ahi tuna.

**Alan Wong**

Alan Wong's
Restaurant
Honolulu, O'ahu

1 garlic clove
1 teaspoon minced fresh rosemary
3 fresh thyme sprigs
1 cup olive oil
4 Maui or other sweet white onions, cut into
    1/4-inch-thick crosswise slices
4 Japanese eggplants, cut into 1/4-inch-thick
    diagonal slices
Salt and freshly ground pepper to taste
8 ounces sashimi-grade 'ahi tuna, cut into 1/4-
    inch-thick vertical slices
4 vine-ripened tomatoes, cut into paper-thin
    slices
8 basil leaves

Put the garlic, rosemary, and thyme in a blender or food processor and purée. With the motor running, gradually add the oil. Set aside. Preheat the broiler. Sprinkle the onions and eggplant on both sides with salt and pepper and place on a dish for 15 minutes to sweat. Pat the vegetables dry with paper towels. Place the vegetables on a grill pan and brush on both sides with the garlic-herb oil. Broil the vegetables 3 inches from the heat until they are lightly browned, about 2 minutes. Refrigerate. Sprinkle the 'ahi with salt and pepper. Heat a large sauté pan or skillet over high heat, coat the pan with the garlic-herb oil, and sear the 'ahi slices for 15 seconds on each side, or until the outside is cooked and the center is still rare. Transfer the 'ahi to a plate and refrigerate.

To assemble ❖ Fan half the tomato slices in a circular pattern around the bottom of a 6-cup bowl lined with plastic wrap. Layer half of the onions, basil leaves, and eggplant at the bottom of the dish. Drizzle with 1 tablespoon of the garlic-herb olive oil. Place half of the 'ahi slices over the vegetables. You may have to cut and piece 'ahi together to form an even layer. Repeat this process to make a second layer of vegetables, infused oil, and seared fish. For the last layer, fan the remaining tomatoes in a circular pattern over the top of the vegetables. Place a small plate upside down on top of the tomatoes and weight with a heavy, small dish or other object. Refrigerate for 1 hour.

To serve ❖ Drain the juices from the 'ahi cake. Unmold the 'ahi cake, carefully slice it into 8 even portions, and serve.

*'Ahi Cake*

# Charred Sichimi 'Ahi Coated with Japanese Spices with Lilikoi-Soy Sauce

Serves 4

Japanese flavors predominate in a simple dish of seared 'ahi with greens. The lilikoi-soy sauce adds the island touch.

**OnJin Kim**

OnJin's Cafe
Honolulu, O'ahu

1/2 Maui or other sweet white onion, finely sliced
1/2 teaspoon fresh lemon juice
1/2 daikon, cut into julienne
1/2 carrot, peeled and cut into fine julienne
12 ounces 'ahi tuna
3 tablespoons shichimi
1/2 tablespoon olive oil

### Lilikoi-Soy Sauce
1 cup dry white wine
1/4 cup unsweetened liliko'i (passion fruit) purée or passion fruit concentrate
1 shallot, sliced
6 white peppercorns
1 bay leaf
1 tablespoon soy sauce
1 tablespoon sugar
1 cup heavy (whipping) cream
1/2 cup (1 stick) unsalted butter, cut into table-spoon-sized pieces

### Garnish
4 shiso leaves, stemmed
4 pieces pickled ginger, drained

Toss the onion with the lemon juice. Place the daikon in cold water to crisp for 15 minutes. Drain the daikon and mix with the carrot. Set aside.

To prepare ❖ the 'ahi

Cut the 'ahi 1-1/2 inches thick, then into rectangles about 6 inches long. Coat the fillets with shichimi. In a heavy, large sauce pan or skillet over high heat, heat the olive oil until just before smoking. Cook a batch of 'ahi for about 10 seconds on each side, or until seared on the outside and rare on the inside. Using a slotted spatula, transfer to paper towels. Repeat to cook the remaining 'ahi. Slice the 'ahi against the grain into 1/8-inch-thick pieces.

<table>
<tr><td>To make<br>the sauce ❖</td><td>In a medium saucepan, combine the white wine, liliko'i purée, shallot, peppercorns, bay leaf, soy sauce, and sugar. If using sweetened passion fruit juice concentrate, omit the sugar.<br><br>Bring to a boil over medium heat and cook until reduced to 1/4 cup. Add the cream and continue to cook to reduce to 1/2 cup. Remove from heat and whisk in the butter, one piece at a time. Keep warm over hot water until ready to use.</td></tr>
<tr><td>To serve ❖</td><td>Place 1/2 teaspoon of the sliced onion in the middle of each plate. Mound 1 tablespoon daikon mixture on top. Place 1 shiso leaf on the top of each plate and set 1 piece of the ginger on the leaf. Ladle 2 tablespoons of sauce around the daikon on the bottom third of each plate. Lean the 'ahi against the daikon on top of the sauce.</td></tr>
</table>

*Charred Sichimi Ahi Coated with Japanese Spices with Lilikoi–Soy Sauce*

# Eggplant Napoleon

Serves 4

Layers of eggplant, herbs, and mozzarella cheese create a savory tower with Italian flavors. The vinaigrette is so good you'll want to make it for other salads.

**David Paul Johnson**

David Paul's
Lahaina Grill
Lahaina, Maui

### Tomato-Balsamic Vinaigrette
1 large tomato, peeled, seeded, and diced
   (page 160)
1/2 cup finely chopped white onion
1/4 cup chopped fresh basil
1/3 cup Dijon mustard
1/3 cup balsamic vinegar
2 tablespoons sugar
1 teaspoon ground pepper
1 teaspoon salt
1 teaspoon Worcestershire sauce
1-1/2 cups olive oil

### Chive-infused Oil
2 garlic cloves
1/4 cup snipped fresh chives
Pinch of kosher salt
3/4 cup olive oil

### Napoleon
1/4 cup olive oil
4 garlic cloves, crushed
2 tablespoons minced mixed fresh herbs
2 large Italian eggplants, cut into 1/8-inch thick
   slices
1 pound mushrooms, thinly sliced
8 ounces smoked mozzarella cheese, thinly
   sliced
1 cup black olives, pitted and finely chopped
1 large Maui or other sweet white onion, finely
   diced
2 red bell peppers, roasted, peeled, seeded
   and diced (page 152)

*continued on the next page*

## Garnish

2 tablespoons chopped mixed fresh opal and
green basil
2 tablespoons grated romano cheese

---

To make
the vinaigrette ❖

In a medium bowl, combine all the ingredients except the oil. Let sit for 10 minutes, then gradually whisk in the oil. If dressing is too thick, add a little cool water. Cover and refrigerate for at least 1 hour.

To make the
chive oil ❖

Put the garlic, chives, and salt in a blender or food processor and purée. With the machine running, add the olive oil in a thin stream. Strain through a fine meshed sieve and pour into a squeeze bottle.

To make the
napoleon ❖

In a small bowl, combine the olive oil, garlic, and herbs. Lightly brush the eggplant with this mixture on both sides. In a large sauté pan or skillet over high heat, sauté the eggplant for 2 minutes on each side, or until browned and crisp. Set aside to cool. Repeat the process with the mushrooms.

To serve ❖

Pool 2 tablespoons of vinaigrette on each salad plate. On each plate, layer ingredients in the following order: eggplant, cheese, olives, onions, bell peppers, and mushrooms. Finish with the eggplant. Sprinkle each with 1/2 tablespoon basil and 1/2 tablespoon romano. Decorate the rim of each plate with chive oil from the squeeze bottle.

*Eggplant Napolean*

**Serves 4**

Poke is a traditional Hawaiian dish usually made with cubes of freshly caught fish eaten raw and seasoned with coarse salt, chilies, and seaweed. Here it gets an update by quickly searing the fish, 'ahi, or skipjack tuna, until it is cooked on the outside and remains rare in the center.

## Sam Choy

Sam Choy's
Restaurants of
Hawai'i
Kailua Kona,
Hawai'i

### Fried Poke
2 teaspoons soy sauce
1/2 cup finely chopped onion
2 teaspoons finely chopped green onion tops
1/2 cup ogo (seaweed)
2 teaspoons Asian sesame oil
10 ounces marlin, cut into
    1-inch cubes

### Keāhole 'Ahi Nori
Four 10-ounce 'ahi tuna steaks, cut into 1/2-by-
    3-inch sticks
Salt to taste
4 teaspoons wasabi paste
2 nori sheets
2-1/2 cups canola oil for deep-frying

### Asian Dressing
4 cups fresh orange juice
1/4 cup black sesame seeds
6 tablespoons sugar
2 tablespoons salt
1 cup canola oil
6 tablespoons plain rice wine vinegar
1/4 cup soy sauce

### Wasabi Vinaigrette
4 cups orange juice
1/4 cup black sesame seeds
6 tablespoons sugar
2 tablespoons salt
1 cup canola oil
6 tablespoons plain rice wine vinegar
1/4 cup soy sauce
1/4 cup wasabi paste
4 handfuls (4 ounces) mixed baby greens

| | |
|---|---|
| To make the ❖ poke | In a medium bowl, combine the soy sauce, onion, green onions, ogo, and 1 teaspoon of the sesame oil. Mix well. Add the marlin and stir to coat. In a wok or skillet over high heat, heat the remaining sesame oil and sear the marlin on all sides for 1 or 2 minutes, or until the outside is opaque and the inside is rare. Transfer the marlin to a plate and set aside. |
| To make the ❖ 'ahi nori | Season the 'ahi sticks with salt and spread wasabi paste on one side of each stick. Cut the nori sheet in half and wrap each fish stick lengthwise. The wasabi paste and moisture from the fish help the nori to adhere. Add 1 inch of oil to a wok or large, deep skillet. Heat the oil to 365°F, or until it sizzles but does not smoke. Add the wrapped fish sticks and cook for about 15 seconds, or until nori is crisp. Using a slotted spoon, transfer the sticks to paper towels to drain. |
| To make the ❖ Asian dressing | Combine all ingredients in a bowl and whisk until incorporated. |
| To make the ❖ wasabi vinaigrette | Combine all ingredients in a bowl and whisk until incorporated. |
| To serve ❖ | Divide the baby greens among 4 plates. Place the fried poke in the center of the greens. Slice the 'ahi nori into pieces and fan around the edges. Drizzle both dressings over the poke and 'ahi nori. |

*Fried Poke with Keahole Ahi Nori*

# Kona Shrimp Lumpia with Spicy Mango Sauce

Serves 6

No appetizer has ever tasted as good as this new twist on the old-fashioned egg roll. Frozen extra-thin lumpia wrappers work well, and you won't be able to get enough of the spicy mango sauce.

**Roy Yamaguchi**

Roy's Restaurant
Honolulu, Oʻahu

## Lumpia Filling
6 ounces cellophane noodles
3 ounces fresh shiitake mushrooms, stemmed and diced, or 1 ounce dried shiitakes, soaked in warm water for 30 minutes
2 tablespoons Asian sesame oil
1 cup finely chopped Chinese mustard cabbage or napa cabbage
1 teaspoon minced fresh cilantro
1 teaspoon minced fresh ginger
1 teaspoon minced garlic
1 green onion, including some of the green top, minced
3 fresh water chestnuts, finely diced
1 pound shrimp, chopped
1 to 2 tablespoons Thai fish sauce (nam pla)
5 tablespoons water
2 tablespoons cornstarch, plus cornstarch for dusting
12 lumpia wrappers

## Spicy Mango Sauce
1/4 cup Thai chili paste or any sweet chili paste
1 cup sake
1/4 cup lilikoʻi (passion fruit) purée, or orange juice concentrate
1/4 teaspoon minced fresh ginger
1/4 teaspoon minced garlic
1 teaspoon minced shallot
1 mango, peeled, cut from the pit, and finely diced

## Garnish
2 teaspoons white sesame seeds, toasted (page 152)
4 teaspoons snipped fresh chives
1/4 mango, peeled, cut from the pit, and cut into julienne

*continue on the next page*

| To make the ❖ lumpia | In a large pot, bring salted water to a boil. Add the noodles and cook for 1 minute, or until just tender. Drain and set aside.

If using dried shiitakes, drain and squeeze them dry, reserving the soaking liquid for another use. Dice the mushrooms. In a skillet over medium-high heat, heat the sesame oil and sauté the mushrooms, cabbage, cilantro, ginger, garlic, green onion, water chestnuts, and cooked noodles for 1 minute. Let cool, then combine with the shrimp and fish sauce.

Mix the water and 2 tablespoons cornstarch in a small bowl. Lay the lumpia wrappers on a work surface and brush the edges of the wrappers with the cornstarch mixture. Place 2 tablespoons filling in a line on the front edge of each wrapper, leaving a 1/2-inch border. Fold the edge of the wrapper nearest you over the filling, then fold in the sides and roll the wrapper into a cylinder. Seal the ends and dust with cornstarch. In a large sauté pan or skillet over high heat, heat the oil until very hot and fry the lumpia, 4 at a time, for about 45 seconds on each side or until golden brown. Repeat with the remaining lumpia. Remove with tongs and drain on paper towels. Keep warm. |

**To make the ❖ mango sauce** — Combine all the ingredients in a medium saucepan. Simmer over low heat for 15 minutes. Strain through a fine-meshed sieve.

Set aside and keep warm.

**To serve ❖** — Pool 1/4 cup of the warm sauce on each of 6 salad plates. Place 2 lumpia on top of the sauce and garnish with the sesame seeds, chives, and mango.

*Kona Shrimp Lumpia with Spicy Mango Sauce*

# Moano and Kahuku Prawns with Moloka'i Sweet Potatoes

Serves 4

Large freshwater Kahuku prawns are farmed on the island of O'ahu and are widely popular with Hawaiian chefs, who often cook them whole, leaving the heads and whiskers on. Moano is reef fish, a member of the goatfish family. Any white fish with a high fat content can be substituted. Callarec likes to leave the skin on to give the dish a distinctive iodine flavor.

**Patrick Callarec**

Chez Paul
Olowalu, Maui

1 tablespoon olive oil
4 Kahuku prawns or jumbo-sized shrimp, shelled
    and deveined
4 2-ounce moano fillets, skin on
Salt and freshly ground pepper to taste
4 Moloka'i sweet potatoes

### Wasabi Aīoli
2 egg yolks
1 garlic clove
Juice of 1/2 lemon
1 tablespoon wasabi powder
1 cup olive oil
Salt and freshly ground pepper

### Lemongrass Bouillabaisse
8 ounces redfish fillet or boned white-fleshed fish
    fillet
3 tablespoons olive oil
1/2 small onion
1 leek, cut into 3-inch lengths, white part only
1/2 celery stalk
1/4 teaspoon cracked peppercorns
1 tomato
1 teaspoon saffron threads
1 garlic clove
1/4 fresh bunch parsley
1/4 fennel bulb
1 fresh thyme sprig
1 bay leaf
1 star anise pod
1/2 stalk lemongrass, white part only
1 kaffir lime leaf
1 teaspoon minced fresh ginger
1/2 cup dry white wine
1 tablespoon Pernod

2 cups fish stock (page 157) or clam juice
1/2 cup heavy (whipping) cream
Salt to taste
3 tablespoons cornstarch mixed with 1/4 cup
    water

In a large sauté pan or skillet over high heat, heat the oil and cook the prawns and fillets on both sides until the prawns are pink, the fillet meat flakes, and the skin is crisp, about 40 seconds on each side. Set aside.

With a sharp knife, carve a 2-1/2-inch-by-2-inch-diameter cylinder out of the center of each sweet potato. Discard the sweet potato parings. Cook the sweet potato cylinders in boiling salted water for 15 minutes, or until tender. With a slotted spoon, remove from the water and drain. Scoop out the center of the potato cylinder with a melon baller. Set aside potato balls for the bouillabaisse.

To make the ❖
aïoli

Put all the ingredients except the oil, salt, and pepper in a blender or food processor and process until frothy. With the machine running, gradually add the oil. Add salt and pepper.

To make the ❖
bouillabaisse

Cut the fish into 1-1/2-inch pieces. In a stockpot over high heat, heat the olive oil, and sauté the fish for 2 minutes, or until it browns lightly on each side. Add the onion, leek, celery, and peppercorns and cook for 4 minutes, or until the vegetables are tender. Add the tomato, saffron, garlic, herbs, spices, wine, and Pernod. Continue to cook until the mixture is reduced to about two-thirds. Add the fish stock or clam juice, and bring to a boil. Reduce heat to simmer and cook until liquid is reduced by one-third. Add the cream and simmer for 5 minutes, or until the cream is completely incorporated into the sauce. Add salt and whisk in the diluted cornstarch. Continue to cook until the cornstarch thickens the sauce.

To assemble ❖

Add the sweet potatoes to the bouillabaisse and simmer to heat through. Place on the plates. Lean 1 fillet and 1 prawn against each sweet potato. Place a spoonful of aïoli in the center of the sweet potato. Drizzle the sauce on and around the fish and sweet potatoes.

*Moano and Kahuku Prawns with*
*Molokai Sweet Potatoes*

# Puna Goat Cheese and Vegetable Terrine

Makes one 8-by-
1/2-inch terrine

Like all good chefs, Ferguson-Ota looks for the finest local products —in this case, goat cheese made in the Puna district of the Big Island. The goat cheese between each layer helps bind this terrine.

**Amy
Ferguson-Ota**

Oodles of Noodles
Kailua Kona,
Hawai'i

3 ounces fresh shiitake mushrooms, stemmed and sliced, or 1 ounce dried shiitakes, soaked in hot water for 30 minutes
6 large Japanese eggplants, sliced lengthwise into 1/4-inch slices
3 large zucchini, sliced lengthwise into 1/4-inch slices
1 medium yellow squash, sliced crosswise into 1/4-inch slices
1 Maui or other sweet white onion, finely diced
12 garlic cloves
Olive oil for brushing and sprinkling
Salt to taste
10 ounces crumbled Puna or other fresh white goat cheese
3 red bell peppers, roasted, peeled, and seeded (page 152)
1 tablespoon chopped basil leaves
1 cup white mushrooms, sliced
1 ripe tomato, peeled and seeded (page 160)
Balsamic vinegar for sprinkling
Freshly ground black pepper to taste
8 sprigs of fresh basil

To make the ❖ terrine

Preheat the oven to 350°F. If using dried shiitakes, drain them, reserving the soaking liquid for another use. Salt the eggplant slices and let sit for 30 minutes; rinse with cold water. Arrange the shiitakes, eggplants, zucchini, squash, onion, and garlic on an oiled baking sheet. Brush with olive oil and sprinkle with salt. Roast for 10 minutes. Set aside and cool. Squeeze half of the garlic cloves out of the skins and chop.

*continued on the next page*

Line a 2-quart loaf pan, terrine, or triangular mold with plastic wrap, leaving 4 inches of plastic wrap hanging over each edge of the pan. Arrange the vegetables in the pan:

Lay the eggplant and zucchini slices across the pan, alternating the vegetables and overlapping the slices to form a continuous layer. Sprinkle with onion. Using your fingers or the back of a spoon, spread a thin layer of cheese on top of the onion. Top with a layer of peppers and a layer of basil. Top with a thin layer of cheese. Sprinkle with mushrooms and the chopped garlic and top with another layer of cheese. Place the squash slices over the cheese. Put the tomatoes over the squash and top with basil. Press down gently with your fingers. Fold the plastic wrap over the top of the mold, and refrigerate for 3 hours.

To serve ❖

Lift the mold out of the pan. Slice through the plastic with a serrated knife. Peel off the plastic and arrange a slice on each chilled plate. Sprinkle with olive oil, balsamic vinegar, and pepper. Garnish with a sprig of basil and the unpeeled roasted garlic cloves.

*Puna Goat Cheese and Vegetable Terrine*

# Seared Lāna'i Venison Carpaccio with Crisp Herb Salad

Serves 4

The venison in this salad is readily available on the island of Lāna'i. If you are unable to get fresh venison, beef tenderloin may be substituted.

**Edwin Goto**

'Ihilani Restaurant at
Mānele Bay Hotel
Lāna'i

### Spice-Rubbed Venison
2 tablespoons sweet paprika
1 tablespoon sugar
2 tablespoons salt
2 tablespoons chili powder
1 teaspoon cayenne pepper
1 teaspoon garlic powder
1 tablespoon ground pepper
8 ounces fresh venison loin

### Mustard Sauce
2 tablespoons whole-grain mustard
1/2 cup crème fraîche or sour cream

### Dressing
1/4 cup olive oil
2 tablespoons plain rice wine vinegar
Salt and freshly ground pepper to taste
Pinch of sugar

### Herb Salad
1 cup toasted croutons (page 147)
1/4 cup fresh chervil leaves
1/4 cup 1-inch pieces fresh chives
1/4 cup fresh flat-leaf parsley sprigs
1/4 cup frisée (curly endive)
1/4 cup coarsely chopped radicchio

### Garnish
1/4 cup finely diced red onion
1/4 cup grated Parmesan cheese

| | |
|---|---|
| To prepare ❖ the venison | In a small bowl, combine the paprika, sugar, salt, chili powder, cayenne, garlic powder, and pepper and mix thoroughly. Roll the venison loin in the spice mixture, coating it thoroughly, and shake off the excess. Heat a dry, heavy, medium skillet over medium-high heat until very hot. Add the venison and sear for 25 or 30 seconds on each side, or until it is evenly browned. Place the loin on a plate and refrigerate for 30 minutes. |
| To make the ❖ mustard sauce | In a small bowl, combine the ingredients and mix well. Cover and refrigerate. |
| To make the ❖ dressing | In a small bowl, whisk the olive oil and vinegar together. Add the salt, pepper, and sugar. Set aside. |
| | Crush the croutons into small pieces in a blender or food processor. Set aside. |
| To assemble ❖ | Remove the loin from the refrigerator and place it on a cutting board. Using a sharp knife, cut it against the grain into 1/16-inch-thick slices. Spread 1 tablespoon mustard sauce into an 1/8-inch-thick layer around the outer edge of each plate. Overlap the venison slices on top of the mustard sauce, completely covering the sauce. Toss the herb salad ingredients with the croutons and the dressing. Arrange the salad on the center of the plate. Sprinkle the red onions and Parmesan around the salad and on top of the venison. |

*Seared Lana'i Venison Carpaccio with Crisp Herb Salad*

# Steamed Seafood Laulau

Serves 4

One of the most traditional of Hawaiian dishes, laulau originally consisted of salted meat and fish wrapped in lū'au leaves (the green tops of the taro plant), then in ti leaves, and steamed in an imu, or underground oven. This updated version is lighter. Aluminum foil, banana leaves, or corn husks may replace the ti leaves.

**Michael Longworth**

Sam Choy's Diamond Head Restaurant Honolulu, O'ahu

### Herb Sauce
1-1/2 cups mayonnaise
1 tablespoon soy sauce
1 tablespoon snipped fresh dill

### Laulau
2 carrots, peeled and cut into fine julienne
2 zucchini, cut into fine julienne
1 cup sliced stemmed fresh shiitake mushrooms
    or dried shiitakes soaked in warm water for
    30 minutes and squeezed dry
8 ti leaves
8 squid, cleaned (page 155)
8 large shrimp, peeled and deveined (page 155)
8 sea scallops
Salt and freshly ground pepper to taste

---

**To make the herb sauce**

Mix the mayonnaise, soy sauce, and dill together and set aside.

**To make the laulau**

Mix the carrots and zucchini together and divide into 4 equal portions. Divide the mushrooms into 4 portions. Remove the hard rib from the ti leaves to make them flexible, or bake on high in a microwave oven for 1 minute to soften. Lay one ti leaf across another at a right angle to form a cross. Or, spread out four 8-inch squares of aluminum foil. Place 1 portion of the carrot mixture in the center of the leaves and top with 2 pieces each of squid, shrimp, and scallops. Add salt and pepper. Spread 1 or 2 tablespoons of the herb sauce in a thin layer on top of the seafood and top with 1 portion of the mushrooms. Gather up the ti leaves, or 4 pieces of aluminum foil, to make a purse and tie with string to make a bundle. Repeat to make 4 bundles. Put the bundles in a steamer or double boiler, cover, and steam over boiling water for 15 minutes.

**To serve**

If using leaves, place each bundle in the center of a plate at the table. If using aluminum foil, remove the steamed food and place in the center of each plate, and top with the cooking juices.

Steamed Seafood Laulau

# Soups and Salads

■ ■ ■

Salads and hot climates go hand in hand. Hawai'i chefs have given the simple green salad new meaning by incorporating crisp wonton wrappers, fiddlehead ferns, and bean thread noodles. The dressings are innovative: the vinaigrettes use such ingredients as sesame oil, chili paste, papaya, and wasabi and can be used on salads and vegetable dishes of your own design.

Island soups are just as fresh and bright, making use of the abundance of island seafood and local vegetables, as in the Hawaiian version of bouillabaisse, and caramelized Maui onion soup.

# 'Ahi and Taro Salad

Serves 4

Raw 'ahi, taro root, macadamia nuts, and a spike of chili pepper water are molded into a colorful salad topped with two colors of tobiko or caviar. A purée of cilantro and macadamia nut oil adds a piquant flavor note.

**Mark Ellman**

Maui Tacos
Lāhainā, Maui

8 ounces taro root, peeled and cut into 1/2-inch cubes

**Cilantro Purée**
4 cups packed fresh cilantro leaves
2 cups macadamia nut oil or walnut oil
Salt and freshly ground pepper to taste
12 ounces sashimi-grade 'ahi tuna, cut into 1/2-inch cubes
1 garlic clove, minced
1/2 Maui or other sweet white onion, minced
1 carrot, chopped
1 beet, peeled and cut into fine julienne
1 cup macadamia nuts, finely chopped
2 teaspoons minced fresh ginger
1 cup soy sauce
2 teaspoons Asian sesame oil
1/4 cup finely chopped ogo (seaweed)
4 teaspoons chili pepper water (page 153)
1/4 cup diced macadamia nuts, toasted (page 151)
4 teaspoons white sesame seeds, toasted (page 152)
1/2 cup black tobiko or salmon caviar
1/2 cup green tobiko

**To cook the taro** ❖ Scrub the outside of the taro root with a brush. Put in a saucepan with enough boiling salted water to cover the taro. Cover and simmer for 1-1/2 hours, or until tender. Remove the taro, drain, and let cool. With a sharp knife, remove the outer peel and cut into cubes.

To make the ❖
cilantro purée

In a blender or food processor, combine the cilantro and oil and purée. Stir in the salt and pepper. Set aside. In a large bowl, combine all the remaining ingredients except the tobiko or salmon caviar. Toss and let sit for 15 minutes. Line a baking pan with parchment paper or aluminum foil. Place four 4-inch ring molds on the prepared baking pan. Divide the salad among the molds and gently pack down to firm. Refrigerate for at least 1 hour.

To serve ❖

Lift the rings with a spatula and place on plates. Run the tip of a small sharp knife around the molds to loosen, and lift the molds Pour one fourth of the purée around each salad mold. Top each salad with a teaspoon of black tobiko and 1/2 teaspoon of green tobiko, or spoon the caviar on top.

'Ahi and Taro Salad

# Caramelized Maui Onion Soup

Serves 4

Maui's sweet white onions are juicier than yellow onions, therefore they cook a little faster. This is a wonderful soup for a cold day. If you are in a hurry, you can substitute canned low-salt chicken broth for the chicken stock.

**David Paul Johnson**

David Paul's
Lāhainā Grill
Lāhainā, Maui

4 large Maui or other sweet white onions, cut
    into thin slices
1 tablespoon sugar
1 teaspoon salt
1/4 cup clarified unsalted butter or olive oil
    (page 140)
1/4 cup dry white wine
1/4 cup dry sherry
2 quarts chicken stock (page 32)
1/4 cup flour mixed with 1/4 cup water
Salt and freshly ground pepper
1/4 cup grated Parmesan cheese
1 cup toasted sourdough croutons (page 147)

In a large bowl, combine the onions, sugar, and salt and stir to mix well. In a large, heavy saucepan over high heat, heat the butter or oil until almost smoking. Add the onions and stir until the onions begin to brown, about 3 minutes. Reduce heat to low and stir until the onions are soft and golden brown. Stir in the white wine and sherry. Set aside.

Return the caramelized onions to the stove and add the strained stock. Bring to a boil, reduce heat to medium, and cook to reduce to about 6 cups. Stir in the flour mixture and return to a boil. Simmer for 5 to 10 minutes. Season and serve with cheese and croutons.

# David Paul's Chicken Stock

Make 8 cups

2 tablespoons olive oil
5 pounds bony chicken parts, skin, and trimmings
1 carrot, chopped
2 celery stalks, chopped
1 large onion, chopped
1 large leek, chopped, white part only
1 cup dry white wine
4 quarts cold water
1 cup port
Assorted fresh herbs tied in a cheesecloth
    square

In a large stockpot over high heat, heat the oil and cook the chicken until it is well browned. Add the vegetables and continue to cook until they soften. Add the white wine, stirring to scrape up the small bits for 2 minutes. Add the cold water, port, and herb packet and bring to a boil. Reduce heat and simmer to reduce to 8 cups. Strain the stock ingredients through a medium-meshed sieve.

*Caramelized Maui Onion Soup*

Serves 4

Spicy and exotic are the best words to describe this colorful and attractive salad. If star fruit is difficult to find, mango makes a wonderful substitute.

**Peter Merriman**

Merriman's Bamboo
Bistro
Wailuku, Hawai'i

1/4 cup olive oil
2 tablespoons minced shallots
2 tablespoons minced fresh cilantro
Salt and freshly ground pepper to taste
16 to 20 large shrimp, peeled with head left on
1 tablespoon minced fresh ginger
1/2 cup fresh lime juice
1/8 teaspoon red pepper flakes
2 tablespoons chopped fresh mint
1 ripe star fruit, sliced thin
4 handfuls (4 ounces) watercress or arugula
    sprigs

In a nonaluminum baking dish, combine the oil, shallots, cilantro, salt, and pepper. Skewer 4 or 5 shrimp on each of 4 sets of parallel skewers, running the skewer through the head and tail of each shrimp and leaving space between shrimp. Marinate at room temperature for 1 hour, or cover and refrigerate for up to 8 hours. Let the shrimp sit at room temperature for 30 minutes before cooking.

Light a fire in a charcoal or gas grill, or preheat the broiler. Combine the ginger, lime juice, pepper flakes, mint, and star fruit in a small bowl; toss to mix. Grill or broil the shrimp for 1 minute on each side, or until pink. Set aside. Make a bed of watercress or arugula on each of 4 salad plates and place one fourth of the star fruit mixture on top of each. Take the shrimp off the skewers and place 4 or 5 on top of each salad.

*Grilled Shrimp and Star Fruit Salad*

**Serves 6**

The Waimānalo district on the island of O'ahu has in recent years become a big producer of fresh gourmet produce. Locals affectionately refer to the area as Nalo. The egg yolks in the vinaigrette can be deleted, if you like. This salad would be delicious with the duck entrée in this book.

**Gerard
Kaleohano**

Mid-Pacific
Country Club
Lanikai, O'ahu

### Crispy Wontons
2 cups peanut oil
1 3-ounce package (24) wonton wrappers,
    cut into julienne

### Tangerine Vinaigrette
6 to 8 egg yolks
3/4 cup whole-grain Dijon mustard
2 tablespoons cider vinegar
2 cups tangerine juice or orange juice
    concentrate
3/4 cup sugar
2 tablespoons salt
1 tablespoon ground pepper
1/4 cup macadamia nut oil or walnut oil

1 head butter lettuce
1 head radicchio
1 head red leaf lettuce
6 cups stemmed Okinawan spinach or arugula
4 chives, snipped
2 tablespoons cider vinegar
1 tablespoon sugar
Salt and freshly ground pepper to taste
1 red bell pepper, seeded, deribbed, and
    diced (page 152)

### Garnish
1 orange, cut into 6 to 8 crosswise slices
1 teaspoon black sesame seeds
6 to 12 edible flowers

In a wok over medium heat, heat the oil until a wonton strip sizzles and rises to the top when submerged. Add the wonton strips and cook until brown and crisp, about 30 seconds to 1 minute. Using a slotted spoon, transfer to paper towels to drain.

In a blender, beat the egg yolks until thickened. Add all the other ingredients except the oil and blend. With the machine running, gradually add the oil to make a smooth sauce.

Tear the lettuce and radicchio leaves into bite-sized pieces. In a large bowl, mix the lettuces and spinach, or arugula.

Submerge the chives in ice water until crisp, about 3 minutes. In a small bowl, combine the vinegar, sugar, salt, and pepper. Add the diced pepper and mix.

Toss the greens with some of the vinaigrette. Swirl vinaigrette on each plate. Mound about 1-1/2 cups of crispy wontons in the center of each plate. Garnish the borders with the bell pepper mixture and orange slices. Arrange the greens on top of the pepper and orange slices. Drizzle more vinaigrette on top if desired. Sprinkle with sesame seeds and garnish with chives and 1 or 2 flowers.

*Nalo Green Salad with Crispy Wontons
and Tangerine Vinaigrette*

# Togarashi Seared Beef Poke with Chilled Spicy Tomato Soup

**Serves 4**

Poke is traditionally a mix of raw diced fish, onions, limu (seaweed), and Hawaiian salt; however, this variation using sautéed beef is very good. If prepared in advance, the flavors have an even better chance to meld into a spicy and delicious dish. Prepared togarashi spice mix, found at Asian markets, can be used if you prefer.

**Thomas B. H. Wong**

The Surf Room
Royal Hawaiian
Waikīkī Sheraton
Honolulu, Oʻahu

**Togarashi Spice Mix**
1-1/2 teaspoons cayenne pepper
1-1/2 teaspoons paprika
1 teaspoon red pepper flakes
1 teaspoon ground pepper
1 teaspoon white sesame seeds, toasted
   (page 152)
1 teaspoon black sesame seeds
1 teaspoon cumin seeds, toasted (page 152)
1 teaspoon mustard seeds, toasted (page 152)

1 pound beef sirloin, cut into 1/2-inch dice
2 tablespoons peanut oil
1/2 Maui or other sweet white onion, diced
1 garlic clove, minced

1 tomato, seeded and diced (page 160)
Minced fresh cilantro to taste
Chili pepper water to taste (page 153)
1 tablespoon soy sauce
1 teaspoon Hawaiian or kosher salt
1 teaspoon patis fish sauce
Chilled Spicy Tomato Soup (recipe follows)

2 green onions, cut into julienne including
   some green tops for garnish

To make the ❖
togarashi spice
mix

Grind all the spice mix ingredients in a spice grinder. Season the beef with the togarashi spice mix. In a sauté pan or skillet over high heat, heat the oil and sauté the beef until it is seared on the outside and rare

*continued on the next page*

on the inside, about 2 minutes. Remove the meat from the pan and refrigerate it for 1 hour. Add all the remaining ingredients except the soup to the seared beef and mix well. Taste and adjust the seasoning.

To serve ❖ Ladle 1/4 of the tomato soup into each dish. Place a portion of the beef poke in the center of the soup and garnish with the green onion.

■ ■ ■

# Chilled Spicy Tomato Soup

1/2 cup olive oil
1 Maui or other sweet white onion, cut into 1/2-inch dice
2 garlic cloves, coarsely chopped
4 vine-ripened tomatoes, quartered
1/2 cup tarragon vinegar
1-1/2 teaspoons chili pepper water (page 153)
3 tablespoons fish sauce, preferably Tiparos® brand

In a saucepan over medium heat, heat 1/4 cup of the oil and sauté the onion and garlic. Add the tomatoes and simmer 2 to 3 minutes, until all the ingredients are tender. Transfer to a blender and purée. With the machine running, gradually add the remaining oil, then the vinegar, chili water, and fish sauce. Cover and refrigerate for 2 to 3 hours before serving.

*Togarashi Seared Beef Poke with*
*Chilled Spicy Tomato Soup*

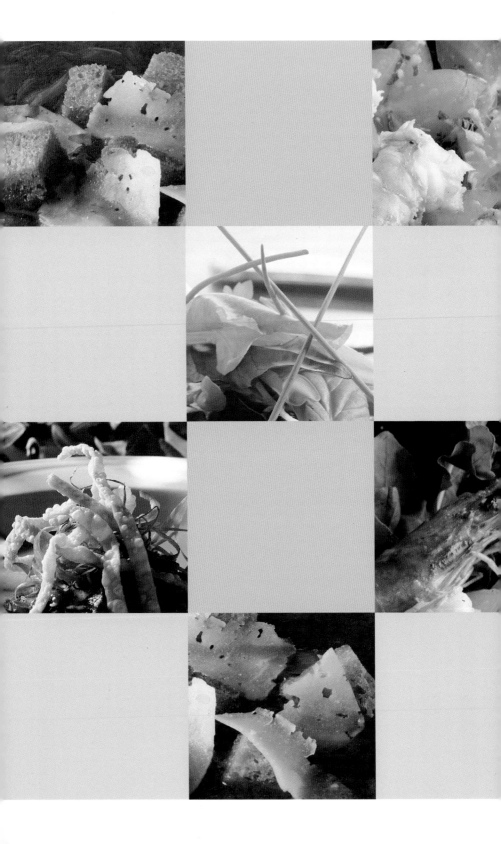

# Poultry and Meats

■ ■ ■

Although fruits and vegetables are playing a larger role in most people's diet and are an important focus for chefs as well, meat and poultry remain favorites with most diners.

Here, you'll find main-course basics with a Hawaiian lilt, like a rack of lamb with Poha Berry and Ginger Butter. New ways to prepare chicken include blackened and Thai-style. And duck gets a Hawaiian treatment with Plum Wine Sauce.

# Beef Tenderloin and Poached Oysters with Essence of Pinot Noir and Chervil Sauce

Serves 4

The silky texture and fresh taste of oysters pair with the perfect beef tenderloins. The rich wine sauce and piquant chervil sauce add the perfect contrasts to this surf-and-turf variation.

**George Mavrothalassitis**

Chef Mavro
Honolulu, Oʻahu

4 tablespoons olive oil
4 6-ounce beef tenderloin fillets
2 bunches spinach, well washed and stemmed
4 large fresh oysters, shucked

**Essence of Pinot Noir**
2 tablespoons olive oil
1 Maui onion or other sweet white onion, finely sliced
1 bottle Pinot Noir wine
1/2 cup carrot, peeled and chopped
Salt and freshly ground pepper to taste

**Chervil Sauce**
2 tablespoons extra-virgin olive oil
1 onion, finely sliced
1 cup dry white wine
1/2 cup minced fresh chervil
Salt and freshly ground pepper to taste

To prepare ❖ the fillets

Preheat the oven to 350°F. In a large sauté pan or skillet over medium-high heat, heat 2 tablespoons of the olive oil and cook the fillets for 3 to 4 minutes on each side. Bake for 6 to 7 minutes for medium rare.

Place the spinach in the top of a steamer and place the oysters on the spinach. Steam the spinach and oysters over boiling water in a medium, covered pot for 3 to 4 minutes, until the oysters have firmed. With a spoon, set the oysters aside on a plate. Drain the spinach well. In a large saucepan over medium heat, heat the remaining 2 tablespoons of olive oil and sauté the spinach for 2 minutes. Set aside.

| | |
|---|---|
| To make the ❖ essence | In a medium saucepan on low heat, heat the olive oil and sauté the onion for 10 minutes. Add one third of the wine and cook to reduce until almost dry. Add another third of the wine and cook to reduce again until almost dry. Add the last third of the wine and cook to reduce by half. Strain, reserving the onion. |
| | In a steamer over boiling water, steam the carrots for 5 minutes, or until tender. Remove and put in a blender or food processor with a little water reserved from the steamer. Purée until smooth. Add the carrot purée to the sauce. Simmer the sauce for 10 minutes. Purée in a blender or food processor until very smooth. Add salt and pepper. |
| To make the ❖ chervil sauce | In a medium saucepan over low heat, heat the olive oil and sauté the onion for 3 minutes, or until translucent. Add the white wine and simmer for 25 minutes. In a food processor or blender, combine the onion mixture and chervil. Purée to a smooth sauce. Add salt and pepper. |
| To serve ❖ | Make a bed of spinach in the center of each plate. Top with a fillet. Top the fillet with one fourth of the reserved onion. Place 1 oyster on the onions. Surround with essence of Pinot Noir and cover the oyster with chervil sauce. |

*Beef Tenderloin and Poached Oysters with*
*Essence of Pinot Noir and Chervil Sauce*

# Blackened Jawaiian Spice Chicken Breasts with Banana-Rum Sauce and Chili Corn Cakes

**Serves 8**

Blackened Jawaiian chicken combines a Caribbean influence with Hawaiian ingredients in this dish. The term Jawaiian comes out of the island surf culture and denotes a blending of Jamaican reggae and Hawaiian influences in food, music, and lifestyle.

**Beverly Gannon**

Hāli'imaile
General Store
Hāli'imaile, Maui

### Jawaiian Spice Mix
2 tablespoons ground allspice
2 tablespoons ground cinnamon
2 teaspoons dried thyme
2 teaspoons dried rosemary
2 teaspoons dried chives
1 teaspoon salt
1 teaspoon sugar
2 teaspoons dried onion
8 boneless skinless chicken breast halves
6 tablespoons clarified butter (page 140)

### Banana-Rum Sauce
2 tablespoons butter
1/2 cup chopped onion
1/2 cup chopped celery
2 garlic cloves, minced
4 bananas, cut into 1/2-inch pieces
2-1/2 cups chicken stock (page 155)
1/2 cup sake
1/2 vanilla bean, halved lengthwise
Juice of 2 limes
3 star anise pods
1/2 cup rum

### Chili Corn Cakes
1-1/4 cups milk
2 tablespoons butter, melted
3 eggs
3/4 cup unbleached all-purpose flour
1/2 cup cornmeal
1/2 teaspoon baking powder
1/2 teaspoon baking soda
1/2 teaspoon salt
1 teaspoon sugar
1 cup fresh or frozen corn kernels
1/2 cup diced peeled green chilies
Peanut oil for frying
Fresh thyme sprigs for garnish

*continued on the next page*

| | |
|---|---|
| To make the ❖ spice mix and blacken the chicken | Combine all the spice ingredients and mix well. Preheat the oven to 350°F. Heat a large cast-iron skillet over high heat until smoking. Coat the chicken breasts with the spice mix. Add to the pan. Drizzle butter over the top of the breasts. Cook for 3 minutes, or until blackened on the bottom. Turn and drizzle more butter on the other side and blacken for another 3 minutes. Bake for about 10 minutes, or until done. |
| To make the ❖ banana-rum sauce | In a medium saucepan, melt the butter over medium heat and sauté the onions and celery for 2 minutes, or until the onion is translucent. Add the garlic and cook for 1 minute. Add the bananas and cook until they begin to caramelize. Add the stock, sake, vanilla bean, lime juice, and star anise, and simmer for 10 minutes. Remove the vanilla bean and star anise. Put the banana mixture into a blender or food processor and purée. Return to the saucepan and add the rum. Cook over medium heat for 2 minutes, or until thickened. Strain through a sieve. |
| To make the ❖ corn cakes | In a large bowl, beat the milk, butter, and eggs together. In a small bowl, stir the flour, cornmeal, baking powder, baking soda, salt, and sugar together. Add the dry ingredients to the wet ingredients. Stir just to combine. Gently blend in the corn and chilies.<br><br>In a large cast-iron skillet over medium heat, heat just enough oil to film the bottom of the pan. Add 1/4 cup batter for each cake. Cook for 1 to 2 minutes on each side, or until golden brown. Repeat to cook the remaining batter. Remove to a plate and keep warm. |
| To serve ❖ | Ladle some sauce onto each plate and place a chicken breast on top. Cut the corn cakes in half and place one half on each side of the chicken. Garnish with thyme. |

*Blackened Jawaiian Spice Chicken Breasts with Banana-Rum Sauce and Chili Corn Cakes*

# Five-Spice Smoked Rack of Lamb with Poha Berry and Ginger Butter

**Serves 4**

The smoked lamb is treated to a fruity, yet spicy poha ginger sauce. Baby green beans provide the perfect touch of crunch and color for this dish.

**Katsuo Sugiura (Chef Suki)**

The Polo Lounge at the Beverly Hills Hotel Beverly Hills, California

**Lamb Marinade**

2 tablespoons peanut oil
8 unpeeled garlic cloves, crushed
1 cup chopped green onions, including some green tops
2 tablespoons sliced fresh ginger
3 cups dry sherry
2 cups water
10 star anise pods
1 cup hoisin sauce
2 teaspoons Chinese five-spice powder
4 tablespoons honey
2 tablespoons Asian sesame oil
1/2 cup soy sauce
2 8-ounce boneless racks of lamb
2 cups (1 ounce) oolong tea leaves
4 cups (2 ounces) sawdust
Peanut oil for frying
1 cup (5 ounces) somen noodles
2 tablespoons olive oil

**Poha Berry and Ginger Butter**

1 cup poha berries, husked
1/2 cup sugar
3 tablespoons fruit-flavored vinegar
1/2 cup dry white wine
2 tablespoons sliced fresh ginger
1 cup veal or beef stock (page 156)
Salt and freshly ground pepper to taste
4 tablespoons cold unsalted butter, cut into tablespoon-sized pieces
2 pounds baby Blue Lake green beans
4 poha berries for garnish

| | |
|---|---|
| To make the ❖ marinade | In a large saucepan, heat the peanut oil and sauté the garlic, green onion, and ginger for 3 minutes, or until the onion is translucent. Add the sherry, water, and star anise and cook for 3 minutes. Add the remaining ingredients and cook for 25 minutes. Let cool. |
| | Pour the marinade into a shallow nonaluminum container. Add the lamb and turn to coat. Marinate for 15 to 30 minutes at room temperature. |
| To smoke the ❖ lamb | Remove the lamb from the marinade, and wipe the excess from the meat. Prepare a smoker according to manufacturer's instructions, using the tea and sawdust in place of wood chips (page 155). Smoke the lamb for 30 minutes. |
| | In a wok or deep fryer, heat the oil to 350°F, or just rippling. With a slotted spoon, lower the somen noodles into the hot oil and fry until brown and crisp. The noodles will rise to the top of the oil. With a slotted spoon, remove the noodles. Drain on paper towels. |
| | Preheat the oven to 350°F. Remove the lamb from the smoker and roll the lamb in the olive oil. Place the lamb in a roasting pan and bake for 25 to 30 minutes, until rare. Crush one half of the fried noodles with your hands and press onto the top of the lamb to make a crust. Reserve the remaining noodles. Cut the lamb into 1/2-inch-thick slices. |
| To make the ❖ poha butter | Purée the berries in a blender or food processor. In a heavy, medium, saucepan, cook the sugar over medium heat until light brown in color. Stir in the vinegar until the sugar dissolves. Add the berry purée, white wine, ginger, and stock. Cook to reduce the mixture by half. Add the salt and pepper. Add the butter and whisk for about 1 minute. |
| To serve ❖ | Spoon some sauce onto each plate. Divide the reserved noodles among the plates and place in the center of the sauce. Fan the lamb slices around the noodles. Place 3 bundles of green beans evenly on each plate, and garnish with a poha berry. |

*Five-Spice Smoked Rack of Lamb with*
*Poha Berry and Ginger Butter*

# Crispy Thai-Style Chicken

Fish sauce is at the heart of Thai cuisine. Ferguson-Ota likes to serve this dish to her family at home with jasmine rice or rice noodles. The chicken marinates overnight, so start a day ahead.

**Amy
Ferguson-Ota**

Oodles of Noodles
Kailua Kona,
Hawai'i

### Marinade
2 heaping tablespoons minced fresh lemongrass
6 large garlic cloves, minced
1 tablespoon grated fresh ginger
2 tablespoons fish sauce, preferably Tiparos®
1 teaspoon Hawaiian or kosher salt
1/2 cup chopped green onions, including some
    green tops
2 tablespoons minced fresh cilantro
1/2 cup mochiko sweet rice flour or all-purpose flour
2 tablespoons cornstarch
2 egg whites
3 pounds boneless skinless chicken breasts or thighs
2 tablespoons peanut oil

### Dressing
1 cup plain rice wine vinegar
1/2 cup water
1/2 cup sugar
1/4 cup fish sauce, preferably Tiparos®
2 Hawaiian or Thai chilies, or sambal olek to taste

### Garnish
4 to 6 handfuls (4 to 6 ounces) mixed baby greens
4 tablespoons minced fresh cilantro
12 fresh cilantro leaves
4 tablespoons basil leaves, shredded

---

To make the ❖
marinade and
chicken

In a large bowl, combine all the marinade ingredients and mix well. Add the chicken and stir to coat. Cover and marinate overnight. Remove from the marinade. In a large sauté pan or skillet over medium-high heat, heat the oil and sauté the chicken for 7 to 10 minutes on each side, or until the meat is opaque throughout and the juices run clear.

To make the ❖
dressing

Combine all the ingredients in a bowl and mix well.

To serve ❖

Serve the chicken on a mound of baby greens. Garnish with herbs and drizzle with the dressing.

Crispy Thai-Style Chicken

# Indonesian Grilled Lamb Chops with Ginger Cream

Serves 4

Kecap manis, a dark, sweet Indonesian soy sauce, gives these lamb chops a unique flavor. The ginger cream and basil purée balance the dish beautifully. The lamb marinates for 24 hours.

**Mark Ellman**

Maui Tacos
Lāhainā, Maui

### Marinade
2 cups kecap manis
2 cups minced peeled fresh ginger
1/4 cup minced garlic
1/4 cup Asian sesame oil
1 cup minced fresh mint
1/2 cup whole-grain mustard
2 pounds lamb loin chops,
      trimmed and sliced

### Ginger Cream
4 cups heavy (whipping) cream
1/2 cup sliced peeled fresh ginger
Salt and freshly ground pepper to taste

### Basil Purée
2 cups fresh basil leaves
2 cups olive oil
Salt and freshly ground pepper to taste
2 roasted garlic cloves (page 154)

### Garnish
8 asparagus tips, blanched
4 tablespoons pickled ginger
White sesame seeds for sprinkling

To make the ❖
marinade

In a shallow nonaluminum container, combine all the marinade ingredients and mix. Add the lamb chops, turn to coat them, cover, and refrigerate for at least 24 hours.

*continued on the next page*

Remove the lamb from the refrigerator 45 minutes before grilling. Light a fire in a charcoal grill or preheat a gas grill. Grill the lamb over a hot fire for 6 to 7 minutes on each side for medium-rare.

To make the ❖
ginger cream

In a small saucepan, combine the cream and ginger. Cook over medium-low heat until reduced by half, or until the mixture coats the back of a spoon. Add salt and pepper. Set aside and keep warm.

To make the ❖
basil purée

Purée all the ingredients in a blender or food processor, in batches if necessary.

To serve ❖

Lace each plate with ginger cream and place one fourth of the lamb chops on top. Sprinkle with asparagus tips and pickled ginger, then drizzle with basil purée and scatter sesame seeds on top.

Indonesian Grilled Lamb Chops with Ginger Cream

# Kālua Duck with Plum Wine Sauce and Lundberg Rice

Serves 4

Moist pieces of duck are placed on top of a rich, nutty rice blend and then drizzled with rich plum wine sauce. The dish gets its name, Kālua Duck, from a traditional preparation for pork: Kālua pig is cooked slowly in an underground oven until it literally falls off the bones.

**David Paul Johnson**

David Paul's
Lāhainā Grill
Lāhainā, Maui

### Kālua Duck
2 ducks, boned and cut into quarters, carcasses and trimmings reserved
2 tablespoons Hawaiian or kosher salt
1 tablespoon ground pepper
8 cups rendered duck fat or vegetable oil (page 154)
1/4 cup liquid smoke (optional)
8 large garlic cloves
1 tablespoon peppercorns

### Plum Wine Duck Sauce
2 reserved duck carcasses and trimmings, above, cut into 1-inch pieces
3 cups finely diced celery
3 cups finely diced carrots
3 cups finely diced onions
2 leeks, white part only, quartered
2 shallots, minced
2 cups Japanese plum wine
2 bay leaves
1 tablespoon peppercorns
4 quarts chicken stock (page 155) or water

### Lundberg Rice
2 tablespoons unsalted butter
1/2 cup minced shallots
1/2 cup minced fresh parsley
1/4 cup Japanese plum wine
2 cups Lundberg rice mix or other wild and brown rice mix
3 cups clarified chicken stock (page 156)

### Steamed Vegetables
8 baby carrots, peeled
8 fresh baby corn
8 baby bok choy

| | |
|---|---|
| To prepare the ❖<br>duck | Preheat the oven to 350°F. Season the ducks with the salt and pepper. Put the ducks in a Dutch oven. In a deep saucepan over medium-high heat, heat the fat or oil to 275°F, or until melted. Add the liquid smoke, if using. Pour over the duck to cover the duck completely. Add the garlic and peppercorns. Cover with a lid and bake for 2 to 3 hours, or until the meat starts to fall off the bones. Let cool to room temperature, then drain off the oil. Remove the meat from the bones. Return the duck and garlic to the pan. |
| To make the ❖<br>plum wine sauce | In a heavy, large pot, brown the duck bones and trimmings over high heat, rendering any fat. Pour off the fat and add the vegetables. Continue to brown, stirring, for 5 minutes. Add plum wine and stir to scrape up the browned bits from the bottom of the pan. Add the bay leaves, peppercorns, and stock or water. Bring to a boil and skim off the fat and foam. Cook over medium heat until reduced by half. Strain, skim the fat, and continue to cook to reduce to 1 or 2 cups of thick sauce. The total reduction time will be about 2 hours. |
| To make the ❖<br>rice | In a heavy, medium saucepan over medium heat, heat the butter and sauté the shallots and parsley until the shallots are translucent, about 3 minutes. Add the wine and stir. Add the rice and sauté for 2 minutes. Add the stock, cover, and reduce heat to a simmer. Cook for 20 minutes, or until the liquid is absorbed. Fluff the rice with a fork and keep warm. |
| To steam ❖<br>the vegetables | Fill the bottom of a steamer with water and bring to a boil. Put the carrots, corn, and bok choy in the top of the steamer and cover. Steam until tender, about 12 minutes. Set aside and keep warm. |
| To serve ❖ | Reheat the duck in the oven on medium heat or in a skillet. Place a mound of rice in the center of each plate and some of the duck on the rice. Circle the sauce around the rice. Cross a baby carrot and a piece of baby corn on each side of the duck. Garnish with the roasted garlic and bok choy. |

Kahua Duck with Plum Wine Sauce and Lundberg Rice

# Fish and Shellfish

■ ■ ■

Thanks to the chefs of the new Hawaiian cuisine and the efforts of the State of Hawai'i, a wide variety of reef and deepwater fish such as opah, kajiki, marlin, shark, and kūmū are now as popular in island cooking as the more familiar onaga, 'ōpaka-paka, and 'ahi tuna. Many of Hawai'i's chefs draw from Asian techniques such as steaming and searing with hot oil, and smoking. Both recipes and techniques are adaptable to stateside fish, and substitutes are given.

Serves 6

Inspired by the heritage of the Upcountry region of Maui, this dish combines clams and sausage with Pacific Rim seasonings of fresh ginger, chili paste, sake, and cilantro.

**Beverly Gannon**

Hāli'imaile
General Store
Hāli'imaile, Maui

2 tablespoons olive oil
1 tablespoon minced garlic
1/2 cup minced fresh ginger
2 onions, finely chopped
3 red bell peppers, seeded, deribbed, and finely chopped (page 152)
8 ounces mild Portuguese sausage (linguiça), cut into 1/4-inch chunks
1-1/2 cups sake
6 cups reduced fish stock (page 157) or clam juice
1-1/2 tablespoons Chinese chili paste
2 tomatoes, peeled, seeded, and coarsely diced (page 160)
5 dozen clams, scrubbed
1/2 cup fresh cilantro sprigs, chopped

In a large pot over medium heat, heat the oil, and sauté the garlic, onions, and red peppers for 2 minutes, or until translucent. Add the sausage and sauté for 5 minutes, or until the sausage is slightly browned. Add the sake and stir to scrape up the browned bits from the bottom of the pan. Add the fish stock or clam broth and cook until reduced by half. Add the chili paste, tomatoes, and clams. Cover and cook until the clams open, approximately 6 to 8 minutes. Discard any clams that do not open. Ladle the clams and broth into bowls and garnish with cilantro.

*Portuguese Steamed Clams*

# Salmon and Shrimp Gyoza with Sweet Chili Vinaigrette and Sweet Chili Beurre Blanc

Serves 4

Gyoza are Japanese fried dumplings, enjoyed alone or with noodles at lunch, dinner, or as a snack. This contemporary version has a filling of salmon and shrimp, and is served with a rich lime-ginger sauce.

**Jean-Marie Josselin**

A Pacific Café
Kapa'a, Kaua'i

### Lime-Ginger Sauce Base
1 cup dry white wine
2-1/2 teaspoons minced fresh ginger
1 cup heavy (whipping) cream
1 cup (2 sticks) cold, unsalted butter, cut into tablespoon-sized pieces
Juice of 1 lime
Salt and freshly ground pepper to taste

### Thai Chili Vinaigrette
3/4 cup olive oil
2 tablespoons mirin or sweet sherry
1/2 cup rice wine vinegar
1 tablespoon minced fresh cilantro
Salt and freshly ground pepper to taste

### Filling
8 medium shrimp
8 to 10 ounces salmon fillet, skinned
1 egg
1/2 cup Thai chili paste
Salt and freshly ground pepper to taste
1/2 red bell pepper, seeded, deribbed, and diced (page 152)
1 fresh cilantro sprig, chopped

### Gyoza
1 tablespoon cornstarch, plus cornstarch for dusting
2 tablespoons water
16 large dim sum or wonton wrappers
Filling, above
1 cup peanut oil for frying
1 tablespoon minced fresh cilantro
1 tablespoon Thai chili paste
4 fresh basil sprigs, stemmed and chopped
1/2 cup extra-virgin olive oil
1 cup shredded Chinese cabbage
2 red bell peppers, seeded, deribbed, and cut into julienne (page 152)
1 fresh cilantro sprig, stemmed and chopped

1/2 cup oyster sauce
1/2 cup Thai chili paste
1 tablespoon minced fresh cilantro
8 fresh flowers

---

**To make the sauce base** ❖ In a medium, heavy saucepan, combine the wine and ginger and bring to a boil. Reduce heat to medium and cook to reduce to about 1/2 cup. Add the cream and cook to reduce to 1 cup. Reduce heat to low and whisk in the butter 1 piece at a time. Remove the pan from heat as necessary to keep the sauce base just warm enough to melt each piece of butter. Add the lime juice, salt, and pepper. Keep warm over tepid water for up to 1 hour.

**To make the vinaigrette** ❖ In blender or food processor, combine all ingredients and purée. Place in a squeeze bottle and refrigerate.

**To make the filling** ❖ Reserve 3 shrimp. In a blender or food processor, combine the salmon, the remaining shrimp, the egg, chili paste, and seasoning. Purée until smooth. Cut the reserved 3 shrimp into small pieces and stir into the mixture with the red bell pepper and cilantro.

**To make the gyoza** ❖ Mix the cornstarch with the water and moisten the edges of the wonton wrappers. Place 1 tablespoon of the filling in the center of a wrapper. With your fingers bring one point across the filling at an angle to the opposite corner, making 2 offset triangles. Grasp both outer points and pull around behind the filling, overlapping slightly. Press the ends together and dust the gyoza with cornstarch. Repeat with remaining wrappers. Bring a large pot of salted water to a boil and drop in the gyoza. Cook for 2 minutes, then remove with a slotted spoon and drain on paper towels.

In a large sauté pan or skillet over medium-high heat, heat the oil to 350°F, or until it ripples. Add the gyoza and cook for 1 minute, until the edges are crisp.

**To finish the sauce** ❖ Put the sauce base, cilantro, and chili paste in a blender or food processor and purée.

In a blender or food processor, combine the basil and oil and purée until smooth. Put in a squeeze bottle.

**To serve** ❖ Pool one fourth of the sauce on a serving plate. Toss the Chinese cabbage, peppers, and cilantro with the Thai chili vinaigrette and mound one fourth in the center of the sauce. Place 4 gyoza in a radial pattern on the greens. Put the oyster sauce and the Thai chili paste in separate squeeze bottles. Drizzle oyster sauce, basil purée, and Thai chili paste over the entire dish. Garnish with a sprinkle of cilantro and 2 fresh flowers. Repeat with remaining dishes.

*Salmon and Shrimp Gyoza with Sweet Chili Vinaigrette and Sweet Chili Beurre Blanc*

# Togarashi-seared Kūmū with Pohole Fern Salad and Sesame Dressing

Serves 4

Kūmū is a local favorite for its delicate flavor. The head is saved to make a rich fish stock. For this warm salad, the pan-seared fillets are stacked on a bed of blanched fern shoots accented with a sauce that blends ginger, soy, and chili flavors.

**Amy Ferguson-Ota**

Oodles of Noodles
Kailua Kona,
Hawai'i

Eight 8-ounce kūmū or red snapper fillets, skin
　　left on one side
Hawaiian or kosher salt to taste
Togarashi to taste
Juice of 2 lemons
1 to 2 tablespoons peanut oil

### Sesame Dressing
1/2 teaspoon minced garlic
1-1/2 tablespoons minced pickled ginger
2-1/2 tablespoons soy sauce
2 tablespoons plain rice wine vinegar
1 teaspoon chili paste
1 teaspoon Asian sesame oil
1 teaspoon snipped fresh chives
1 teaspoon sugar

### Fern Salad
1 pound fiddlehead ferns (pohole), blanched,
　　or haricots verts or baby Blue Lake green
　　beans
4 handfuls (4 ounces) mixed baby greens
1 small Maui or other sweet white onion, cut
　　into 1/4-inch strips
2 tomatoes, seeded, peeled, and cut into
　　1/4-inch strips (page 160)

### Garnish
1 tablespoon paprika
4 teaspoons togarashi
4 teaspoons snipped fresh chives

*continued on the next page*

| To prepare the fish | Score the fillets about 1/2 inch deep so they will not curl when fried. Use pliers to pull any visible bones from the fillets. Season with the salt, togarashi, and lemon juice. In a large sauté pan or skillet over high heat, heat the peanut oil and sear the fish for 1 minute on each side, or until opaque throughout. Set aside and keep warm. |
| To make the salad | Whisk all the dressing ingredients together. Combine all the salad ingredients and toss with the dressing. |
| To serve | Lightly dust the rim of the plate with paprika. Pile salad in the middle of each plate. Top with the tomato strips. Lean 2 fillets against the greens on each plate, skin-side in. Drizzle dressing around the edges of the plate and sprinkle with togarashi and chives. |

*Togarashi-seared Kūmū with Pohole Fern
Salad and Sesame Dressing*

# Roasted 'Ōpakapaka with Orange-Ginger Butter Sauce

Serves 4

When French technique meets fresh island fish, you get a refreshing dish like this roasted 'ōpakapaka. Cradled in purée and orange sections, the fish is moist and bright with island flavor.

**Gerard Reversade**

Gerard's at the Plantation Inn Lāhainā, Maui

1 whole 'ōpakapaka or other mild white-fleshed fish, about 2-1/2 pounds
Salt and freshly ground pepper to taste
2 tablespoons extra-virgin olive oil
1 small bunch fresh savory
1 Hawaiian or Thai chili, seeded and chopped, or 1 pinch of red pepper flakes
1/2 orange, cut in 1/4-inch slices

**Potato-Carrot Purée**
2 large potatoes, peeled and coarsely chopped
1 carrot, peeled and coarsely chopped
4 tablespoons unsalted butter
Salt, ground nutmeg, and white pepper to taste

**Orange-Ginger Sauce**
1/4 cup water
1/2 cup (1 stick) unsalted butter, cut into pieces
2 teaspoons minced fresh ginger
1 Hawaiian or Thai chili, seeded and minced, or 1 pinch of red pepper flakes
Juice from 1 orange
1 orange, sectioned and seeded
2 green onions, green tops only, chopped

To prepare ❖ the fish

Preheat the oven to 450°F. Place the whole fish on a work surface. With a sharp knife, score the fish in a criss-cross pattern on each side. Sprinkle the fish cavity with salt and pepper. Fill the cavity with the savory and chili, and top the fish with orange slices. In a large ovenproof sauté pan or skillet over high heat, heat the olive oil and add the fish. Cook for 30 seconds on each side, then place the fish in the oven and bake for 25 to 30 minutes, or until the meat flakes but is still moist.

| | |
|---|---|
| To make the ❖ <br> purée | In a medium saucepan of salted, boiling water, cook the carrots and potatoes until tender, about 25 minutes. Drain and put the vegetables in a blender or food processor with the butter and seasonings. Purée. Set aside and keep warm. |
| To make the ❖ <br> sauce | Add the water to a small saucepan and bring to a boil. Gradually add the butter, then the ginger, chili, and orange juice. |
| To serve ❖ | Arrange the fish on a platter. Place the purée in a large pastry bag fitted with a large star tip and pipe curving swirls of purée on each side of the fish. Pour the butter sauce over the top and arrange the orange sections around the outside. Sprinkle the top of the fish with the green onions. |

*Roasted ʻŌpakapaka with Orange-Ginger Butter Sauce*

# Jasmine Tea-steamed Fillet of 'Ōpakapaka with Coriander-Butter Sauce

**Serves 4**

Ginger brightens the crust on these fish fillets, coated with a silken cream reduction sauce. The simple but intensely flavored dish is garnished with a pick-up-sticks design of julienned carrot and green onion.

**Russell Siu**

3660 on the Rise
Honolulu, O'ahu

Four 5-ounce 'ōpakapaka fillets
Salt and freshly ground pepper to taste
1 cup fresh bread crumbs
1 tablespoon grated fresh ginger
2 large fresh cilantro sprigs, stemmed and
    minced (stems reserved)
3 cups water
2 jasmine tea bags

### Coriander-Butter Sauce
1-1/2 tablespoons coriander seeds
2 tablespoons dry white wine
2 tablespoons plain rice wine vinegar
Reserved cilantro stems, above
1/4 cup heavy (whipping) cream
1 cup (2 sticks) unsalted butter, cut into
    tablespoon-sized pieces
Salt and freshly ground pepper to taste

### Garnish
2 cups julienned green onions
1 carrot, peeled and cut into julienne
1 teaspoon finely diced fresh ginger

To prepare ❖
the fish

Sprinkle the fish with salt and pepper. In a small bowl, combine the bread crumbs, ginger, and chopped cilantro. Sprinkle this mixture over the fish. Put the fish in the top part of a steamer. In a small saucepan, bring the water to a boil. Set aside, add the tea, and steep for 3 minutes. Pour the tea into the bottom of the steamer, discarding the tea bags. Bring to a simmer, add the steamer section, cover, and steam for about 12 minutes, or until the fish flakes easily. Remove the fish from the pan and keep warm.

*continued on the next page*

To make the ❖
sauce

In a heavy, medium saucepan, combine the coriander seeds, white wine, vinegar, and cilantro stems. Cook over medium-high heat until reduced by half. Reduce heat to medium, add the heavy cream, and cook to reduce by half again. Reduce heat to low and whisk in the butter 1 tablespoon at a time. Strain through a fine-meshed sieve and season with salt and pepper.

To serve ❖

Place 1/4 cup of sauce on each plate and place 1 fillet in the center. Garnish the top of the fish with green onions and carrot, and sprinkle the ginger over the plate.

*Jasmine Tea-steamed Fillet of ʻŌpakapaka*
*with Coriander-Butter Sauce*

# Sautéed Shrimp and Penne with Rice Cream Sauce

**Serves 4**

Penne pasta are topped with a creamy rice-based sauce studded with beautiful seared shrimp. The ingenious Alfredo-style sauce is made without cream, and the only butter is used as an enrichment for the shrimp. You may cut the quantity of the butter if you wish.

**Alan Wong**

Alan Wong's
Restaurant
Honolulu, O'ahu

### Rice Cream Sauce
1 cup long-grain white rice
5-1/2 cups fish stock (page 157) or clam juice
2-1/2 cups water
1 tablespoon olive oil
1 tablespoon minced garlic
1 tablespoon minced shallot
3/4 cup tomato water (recipe following)
1 cup dry white wine
4 cups chicken stock (page 155)
1-1/2 tablespoons salt
24 large shrimp, peeled and deveined, tails
    left on
Salt and freshly ground pepper to taste
Flour for dredging
1/2 cup olive oil
2 teaspoons minced garlic
1/2 cup dry white wine
3/4 cup tomato water (recipe following)
2 teaspoons capers, drained
1/2 cup finely diced tomatoes
1/2 cup garlic-herb butter (page 141)
4 tablespoons minced fresh Italian parsley
20 ounces penne pasta

### Garnish
8 tablespoons grated Parmesan cheese
4 fresh basil sprigs
2 tomatoes, peeled, seeded, and chopped
    (page 160)

Wash the rice. In a large saucepan, combine the rice, fish stock or clam juice, and water. Bring to a boil, then reduce heat to low and cook for 30 to 45 minutes, or until the liquid is absorbed and the rice is soft. Purée the rice in a blender or food processor until smooth.

In a large saucepan over medium-high heat, heat the oil and sauté the garlic and shallots for 2 minutes, until lightly browned and slightly translucent. Add the tomato water and white wine. Boil the mixture for 2 minutes, then add the chicken stock. When the stock boils, reduce heat to low and stir in the puréed rice. Add the salt and set aside.

Sprinkle the shrimp with salt and pepper and dredge lightly in flour. In a large sauté pan or skillet over medium-high heat, heat the olive oil until it ripples. Add the shrimp and sauté for 30 seconds on each side, or until golden. Add the garlic, wine, and tomato water, and stir to scrape up the browned bits from the bottom of the pan. Add the capers, tomatoes, garlic butter, parsley, and rice cream sauce. Cook and stir until the liquid has evaporated, 5 to 7 minutes. Season with salt and pepper.

Cook the pasta in a large pot of salted boiling water until al dente. Drain and toss with the shrimp sauce.

To serve ❖   Divide among 4 shallow bowls. Garnish each with 2 tablespoons of cheese and a basil sprig. Place a tablespoon of chopped tomato over center of each.

■ ■ ■

# *Tomato Water*

8 vine-ripened tomatoes
Pinch of salt

With a sharp, small knife, cut the unpeeled tomatoes into chunks. Sprinkle with a pinch of salt and toss. Place the tomato chunks in a fine-meshed sieve over a bowl, or wrap in cheesecloth and place in a colander over a bowl. Refrigerate overnight and let drip. A clear tomato liquid will collect in the bowl. The tomato water may be used for subtle flavoring; keep in a covered jar in the refrigerator up to 5 days.

*Sautéed Shrimp and Penne with Rice Cream*
*Sauce and Butter Sauce*

# Papillotte of Kūmū with Basil, Seaweed, and Shiitake Mushrooms

Serves 4

Kūmū is a small member of the goatfish family, and like its cousins moano and weke, it's often fried whole. Steaming in parchment paper allows the fish to make its own sauce, enhanced by a surprising combination of ingredients.

**George Mavrothalassitis**

Chef Mavro
Honolulu, Oʻahu

4 tablespoons extra-virgin olive oil
8 ounces shiitake mushrooms, stemmed and sliced
1 cup thinly sliced Maui or other sweet white onions
1-1/2 pounds kūmū or red snapper fillets, skin on
1 cup ogo (seaweed)
4 fresh basil sprigs, stemmed and minced
1/4 cup dry white wine
1/4 cup olive oil
1/4 cup fish stock (page 157), or clam juice mixed with 1/4 cup water
Salt and freshly ground pepper to taste
1 egg yolk, beaten

In a medium sauté pan over medium-high heat, heat 2 tablespoons of the oil and sauté the mushrooms for 2 minutes, or until lightly browned on the edges. Remove the mushrooms from the pan and set aside. Heat the remaining oil in the pan and sauté the onions for 2 minutes, or until translucent. Set aside.

Preheat the oven to 450°F. Cut the fish into eight 1-inch-thick pieces. Cut 4 circles of parchment paper 14 inches in diameter. Fold the paper in half to make a center crease. Open the paper toward you and arrange the ingredients in the center: On 1 paper circle, layer one fourth of the onions, 2 fillets, and one fourth each of the mushrooms, ogo, basil, white wine, olive oil, and diluted fish stock. Salt and pepper to taste. Repeat with remaining 3 circles. Brush the inner edge of the paper with the beaten egg and fold the paper in half over the ingredients. Beginning at the crease, fold the cut edges upward and back over themselves in 2-inch sections, sealing as you work and forming a twisted edge. Paper clip the final twist to hold tightly. It will look like a large tart.

Place the papillottes in a large, dry, ovenproof skillet over medium-high heat just until they begin to puff. Place the skillet in the oven and bake for 8 minutes. The parchment will puff slightly. With scissors, cut an opening in the parchment paper to allow the steam to escape. Serve the packages at the table.

*Papillotte of Kūmū with Basil, Seaweed, and Shiitake Mushrooms*

# Wok Lobster with Lehua Honey and Black Bean Sauce

Serves 4

Although it looks elegant, this is a simple and quick dish to prepare. It is served family-style on a platter. The thick and fragrant lehua honey featured in the dish is made from the nectar of a plant that grows on the side of Maui's volcano.

**Patrick Callarec**

Chez Paul
Olowalu, Maui

### Lehua Honey and Black Bean Sauce
1 teaspoon cornstarch
1/2 cup water
1 cup Chinese fermented black beans, rinsed and chopped
1 teaspoon sesame oil
1 teaspoon coconut oil
1 teaspoon minced garlic
1 teaspoon minced fresh ginger
1/2 teaspoon minced lemongrass
1 teaspoon minced green onion (white portion only)
1 teaspoon minced fresh cilantro
1 teaspoon grated orange zest
1 teaspoon chili paste
1 teaspoon soy sauce
1 teaspoon oyster sauce
1 teaspoon lehua honey or other fragrant honey
1-1/2 cups chicken or fish stock (page 157) or clam juice
Two 2-pound Maine lobsters or 4 rock lobster tails
1 teaspoon sesame oil
1 teaspoon peanut oil

### Noodles
One 12-ounce package fresh Chinese egg noodles
2 tablespoons sesame oil
2 tablespoons peanut oil

### Garnish
1 teaspoon julienned green onions
4 fresh cilantro stems
6 orange zest strips

*continued on the next page*

In a small bowl, dissolve the cornstarch in the cold water and set aside. Coarsely chop half of the black beans. In a large wok over medium heat, heat the oil to rippling and stir-fry the chopped and whole beans, garlic, ginger, lemongrass, green onion, and cilantro until the vegetables are wilted. Add the zest and chili paste, and stir-fry for 1 minute. Stir in the soy sauce, oyster sauce, honey, and stock or clam juice. Bring to a boil and pour in the cornstarch mixture, stirring until thickened. Simmer for 15 minutes. Remove from heat.

Bring a large pot of water to a boil. Kill the lobsters by making an incision in the back of the shell where the chest and tail meet. Immediately add the lobsters to the boiling water for 2 minutes. Using tongs, remove the lobsters and drain on paper towels. Place on a cutting board and cut the tail from the body where they join. Cut the tail into 3/4-inch slices, keeping the meat inside the shell. Cut the claws away close to the body and cut the knuckles away at the claws, keeping the claws intact. Remove the legs. Pull the meat from the knuckles and crack the claws, removing the lower part of the shell to expose the meat. If using lobster tails, cut into medallions, keeping the meat inside the shell.

In a clean wok over high heat, heat sesame and peanut oils until rippling. Add the lobster and stir-fry for 1 minute. Add to the wok with the black bean sauce, cover, return to medium heat, and cook for 2 minutes. Remove from heat.

To make the ❖
noodles

Bring a large pot of water to a boil and add the noodles. Cook for 7 minutes, then drain well and pat dry with a paper towel. In a large wok over high heat, combine 1 tablespoon sesame oil and 1 tablespoon peanut oil and heat to rippling. Put the noodles in the oil, shaping them into a cake with the back of a spoon. When the cake has turned a golden color on one side, about 2 minutes, turn it with a large spoon or spatula and reshape into a cake. Pour 1 tablespoon sesame oil and 1 tablespoon peanut oil around the edges of the cake and cook until golden brown on the second side, about 2 minutes.

To serve ❖

Place the noodle cake in the center of a large platter. Split the body of the lobster in half lengthwise. Arrange all the lobster pieces or tails over and around the noodles. Pour the black bean sauce over and around the lobster. Garnish with green onions, cilantro sprigs, and orange zest.

*Wok Lobster with Lebua Honey and Black Bean Sauce*

Serves 4

The Japanese bread crumbs called panko make this dish very "island" in flavor, and the coconut, spinach, and crabmeat in the bisque make it taste like a lū'au. The bisque is made of puréed taro leaves enriched with cream and coconut milk, forming a rich green halo around the fish.

**Sam Choy**

Sam Choy's
Restaurants of
Hawai'i
Kailua Kona,
Hawai'i

### Mashed Purple Sweet Potatoes
1 pound Okinawan or regular
    sweet potatoes
1 cup hot milk
1 tablespoon unsalted butter
Salt and freshly ground pepper to taste

### Crab Bisque
4 tablespoons unsalted butter
2 onions, diced
2 tablespoons flour
2 cups heavy (whipping) cream
1 cup coconut milk
2 cups green taro leaves or frozen spinach,
    chopped
1-1/2 cups fresh lump crabmeat
Salt and freshly ground pepper to taste

### Crusted Mahimahi
1 cup panko (Japanese bread crumbs)
1 cup macadamia nuts, finely chopped
1/2 cup minced fresh parsley
Four 8-ounce mahimahi fillets
Salt and freshly ground pepper to taste
1/2 cup all-purpose flour
2 eggs, lightly beaten
1/4 cup vegetable oil for frying

### Sautéed Vegetables
2 tablespoons peanut oil
1 cup finely chopped onions
1 cup fresh bean sprouts
1/2 cup diagonally cut celery
5 ounces shiitake mushrooms, stemmed and
    sliced
3 ounces white mushrooms, sliced
1 red bell pepper, seeded, deribbed, and cut
    in julienne

**Garnish**
2 fresh cilantro sprigs
1 tablespoon black sesame seeds

---

To make the ❖
potatoes

Peel the sweet potatoes and cut into 1-inch dice. Cook the sweet potatoes in salted boiling water until tender, about 6 minutes. Drain. Combine the milk and butter and stir until the butter melts. Mash the potatoes with a masher or beater. Beat in the milk mixture. Add salt and pepper. Set aside and keep warm.

To make the ❖
crab bisque

In a large saucepan, melt the butter and sauté the onions until translucent, about 3 minutes. Stir in the flour and blend well. Add the heavy cream and simmer for 5 minutes, stirring frequently. Stir in the coconut milk, taro or spinach, and crabmeat. Add salt and pepper. Reduce the heat to low and cook until the mixture thickens slightly.

To make the ❖
crusted
mahimahi

In a shallow bowl, combine the panko, macadamia nuts, and parsley. Season the mahimahi with salt and pepper and dust with flour. Dip each fillet in the eggs, then the macadamia nut crust mixture, to coat on both sides. In a large sauté pan or skillet over medium-high heat, heat the oil and cook the mahimahi for 2 minutes on each side, or until golden brown.

To make the ❖
vegetables

In a medium sauté pan or skillet over medium-high heat, heat the oil and sauté the onions until translucent, 3 minutes. Add the remaining ingredients, reduce heat to medium, and sauté until tender, 3 to 5 minutes. Set aside and keep warm.

To serve ❖

Put the mashed potatoes in the center of the serving platter. Place the crusted mahimahi fillets on top of the potatoes. Spoon the vegetables on one side of the plate. Pour the bisque completely around the fillets and vegetables. Garnish with cilantro sprigs and sesame seeds.

*Crusted Mahimahi with Crab Bisque*

# Sautéed Mahimahi on Stir-fried Watercress with Ginger Beurre Blanc and Noodle Cakes

Serves 6

A mixture of French, Japanese, and Thai styles results in a dish that is creamy smooth with the sharp bite of peppers. Soba noodle cakes and curried stir-fried vegetables serve as a base for delicate mahimahi fillets and a ginger beurre blanc. Adjust the heat with the peppers, ginger, and chili sauce.

**Peter Merriman**

Merriman's
Restaurant
Waimea, Hawai'i

### Curry Sauce
2 tablespoons grated galangal or fresh ginger
3 lemongrass stalks, white part only
4 kaffir lime leaves, chopped
1 shallot
4 garlic cloves
2 tablespoons Thai chili paste

### Ginger Beurre Blanc
1-1/2 cups dry white wine
2 tablespoons minced shallots
3 fresh parsley sprigs
3 white mushrooms, chopped
1/4 cup pickled ginger, cut into julienne
2 tablespoons heavy (whipping) cream
1 cup (2 sticks) unsalted butter, cut into table-
    spoon-sized pieces
Salt and freshly ground pepper to taste

### Noodle Cakes
2 pounds soba noodles
1/2 cup extra-virgin olive oil for frying
Six 6-ounce mahimahi fillets
Salt and freshly ground pepper to taste
1 cup cornstarch
1/4 cup extra-virgin olive oil

### Spicy Stir-fried Vegetables
1 tablespoon Curry Sauce, above
1 red bell pepper, seeded, deribbed, and cut
    into julienne
1/4 cup white mushrooms, quartered
1/2 Maui or other sweet white onion, cut into
    julienne
1/4 bunch watercress, stemmed
1/2 cup fresh bean sprouts
1/4 cup Thai fish sauce

*continued on the next page*

**Garnish**
2 tablespoons unsalted peanuts, chopped
1/4 cup fresh cilantro leaves, chopped

---

To make the ❖
curry sauce

Grind all ingredients in a blender or a food processor until smooth. This can take 8 minutes or longer. Reserve or freeze until ready to use.

To make the ❖
beurre blanc

In a medium saucepan, combine the wine, shallots, parsley, mushrooms, and half of the pickled ginger. Cook over medium heat until almost evaporated. Add the cream and cook to reduce by half. Reduce heat to low and whisk in the butter 1 piece at a time. Remove the pan from the heat as necessary to keep the sauce just warm enough to melt each piece of butter. Remove from the heat and strain through a fine-meshed sieve. Add the remaining ginger, salt, and pepper. Keep warm over tepid water.

To prepare the ❖
noodle cakes

Bring a large pot of water to boil over high heat. Add the noodles and let boil until just soft to the bite, about 6 minutes. Drain in a colander. Divide the noodles into 6 equal portions. In a large sauté pan or skillet over medium-high heat, heat the oil until rippling. Add noodles, one portion at a time, pressing into a rectangle with the back of a spoon as they cook until they hold their shape. Cook on both sides until crisp and golden brown, about 3 minutes per side. Remove with a slotted spoon and drain on paper towels; set aside and keep warm. Repeat with remaining noodle portions.

Sprinkle the fillets with salt and pepper and coat them with cornstarch. In a large sauté pan or skillet over medium-high heat, heat the oil and cook the fillets for 3 minutes on each side, or until they flake easily and are golden brown.

To make the ❖
stir-fried
vegetables

Heat a wok over high heat, add the curry sauce, and stir-fry for 30 seconds. Add the bell pepper, mushrooms, onion, and watercress. Stir-fry for 1 minute. Add the bean sprouts and fish sauce. Set aside and keep warm.

To serve ❖

Place the noodle cakes at one end of a serving platter. Spoon the vegetables down the center of the platter, moving the red pepper strips to the top center of the vegetables. Spoon the beurre blanc over the vegetables, letting the sauce pool on the platter. Place 3 fillets on each side of the vegetables, touching in the center. Sprinkle with the peanuts and cilantro.

Sautéed Mahimahi on Stir-fried Watercress
with Ginger Beurree Blac and Noodle Cakes

# Pan-seared Onaga Fillet with Pumpkin and Curry Sauce

Serves 4

Local vegetables stir-fried with green curry sauce add spicy heat to the creamy smoothness of seared, baked onaga. This is a good company dish: The curry paste and vegetable preparation can be done ahead of time, the onaga is ready after just a few minutes of preparation, and the vegetables are stir-fried at the last minute. Adjust the heat with the number of chilies used.

**Steve Amaral**

Kea Lani Hotel
Suites & Villas
Wailea, Maui

**Green Curry Paste**
2 shallots
2 garlic cloves
1/2 cup peanut oil
10 small green Thai chilies
10 coriander seeds, ground
10 cumin seeds, ground
10 black peppercorns
2 lemongrass stalks, white part only, chopped
1 inch galangal or fresh ginger, peeled and sliced
4 green onions, green part only, chopped
2 bunches fresh cilantro
10 kaffir lime leaves
10 fresh lemon basil leaves
3 kaffir lime zest strips

Four 6-ounce onaga or red snapper fillets,
    each 1-1/4 inches thick
3/4 cup peanut oil
Salt and freshly ground pepper to taste

**Vegetables**
1/2 kabocha pumpkin or butternut squash, or
    1 acorn squash
2 Yukon Gold potatoes
1 Japanese or Italian eggplant
2 tablespoons peanut oil
Salt and freshly ground pepper to taste
1 leek, cut into fine julienne
1 carrot, peeled and cut into fine julienne
2 green onions, green part only, cut into julienne

### Curry Sauce

2 tablespoons peanut oil
2 lemongrass stalks, white part only, cut into
    4-inch lengths
2 green Thai chilies, minced
1 inch galangal or fresh ginger, peeled and
    julienned
4 kaffir lime leaves
1 cup bamboo shoots, julienned
6 fresh basil sprigs
12 fresh cilantro sprigs
1/3 cup coconut milk
1/3 cup chicken stock (page 155)
Green Curry Paste, above
Vegetables, above
Salt and freshly ground pepper to taste
Fish sauce to taste, preferably Tiparos®
Date palm or raw sugar to taste

### Garnish

1 cup peanut oil
Blanched leeks, carrots, and green onions,
    above

To make the ❖
curry paste

Put all ingredients in a blender or food processor and blend until smooth. Set aside.

To prepare ❖
the fish

Cut each fillet crosswise into four 1-1/2-inch-thick slices. In an ovenproof nonstick or seasoned cast-iron skillet over high heat, heat the oil until almost smoking. Sear the fish for 1 minute on each side, until crisp. Season with salt and pepper. Set aside and keep warm.

To prepare ❖
the vegetables

Cut the pumpkin or squash, potato, and eggplant into 1-inch cubes and coat with the oil. Season with salt and pepper, put in a roasting pan, and bake for 15 to 20 minutes, or until three-fourths cooked. Let cool to room temperature. (The vegetables will continue to cook as they cool.) Drain again and set aside.

*continued on the next page*

Blanch the leek, carrot, and green onions in boiling water for 30 seconds. Drain and plunge into ice water. Set aside.

To make the ❖
curry

In a wok over high heat, heat the oil and stir-fry the lemongrass, chili, ginger, lime leaves, and bamboo shoots for 1 minute. Add the basil and cilantro, and stir-fry for 1 minute. Reduce heat to medium and add the coconut milk, stock, curry paste, and vegetables. Add the remaining ingredients and simmer for 2 to 3 minutes.

To make the ❖
garnish

Remove the leeks, carrots, and green onions from the water and scramble them together. Divide the vegetable scramble into fourths. Drain until nearly dry on paper towels. In a deep fryer or wok over high heat, heat the oil to smoking. In a frying basket or with a slotted spoon, lower one tangle of vegetables into the hot oil and fry for 15 seconds. Remove and drain on paper towels. Repeat with the remaining tangles.

To serve ❖

Place 1 fillet in a corner of each plate. Top the fish with curried vegetables. Place a tangle of fried vegetables on top of each serving.

*Pan-seared Onaga Fillet with Pumpkin and Curry Sauce*

# 'Ōpakapaka with Sesame-Chili Sauce

**Serves 4**

A halo of fresh asparagus and a flavorful sauce made with ginger and chili make a healthful dish look and taste spectacular. At heart, this is a simple fillet of perfectly cooked fish.

**OnJin Kim**

OnJin's Cafe
Honolulu, O'ahu

24 asparagus stalks
Four 6-ounce 'ōpakapaka or other mild white-
    fleshed fish fillets
1/2 cup Asian sesame oil
1 teaspoon minced fresh ginger
1 Hawaiian or Thai chili, finely diced, or
    1 pinch of red pepper flakes
2 tablespoons finely chopped green onion,
    white part only
1/4 cup soy sauce
8 fresh cilantro sprigs, stemmed

---

Holding an asparagus stalk in your hands, bend it until it snaps off. Discard the tough lower end. With a sharp, small knife, score the skin of the fish in a criss-cross pattern. Place the asparagus and 'ōpakapaka over simmering water in a covered steamer for 5 minutes, until the fish is opaque on the outside but translucent in the center. The asparagus will be crisp-tender.

In a sauté pan or skillet over high heat, heat the oil and sauté the ginger, chili, and 1 tablespoon of the green onions for 12 seconds. Add the soy sauce and bring to a boil.

**To serve** ❖

Place a fillet in the center of each serving plate. Pour the sauce over the fish fillets. Place 6 asparagus stalks single file around each plate, overlapping the tip of one over the lower end of the next. Garnish the fish with the cilantro sprigs and remaining 1 tablespoon green onion.

'Ōpakapaka with Sesame-Chili Sauce

# Desserts

■ ■ ■

Island desserts make use of the Hawaiian cornucopia of tropical fruits: guava, coconut, star fruit, kiwi, papaya, pineapple, mango, banana, and lemon, and such exotics as liliko'i (passion fruit) and poho berries (Cape gooseberries). There's plenty of chocolate for those who think dessert's not dessert without it: A flourless chocolate cake laced with macadamia nuts and Hawaiian Vintage Chocolate whipped in a ganache.

Admittedly, many of the desserts are complex examples of the professional chef's art. They are painstakingly explained, step-by-step. In quite a few cases, the most complicated part of the dessert is the garnish, so you can simplify these by omitting that element, or using only one part of the garnish. Other desserts are easy and quick to prepare like Mark Ellman's Caramel Miranda.

Serves 8

The aromatic flavorings of each kind of brûlée must infuse in the cream, so each combination is brought to a very slow simmer before being added separately to egg yolks and sugar. The reward is five exotic flavors and a stunning presentation of a much-loved dessert.

**Mark Okumura**

Alan Wong's
Restaurant
Honolulu, O'ahu

### Kona Mocha Crème Brûlée

1-1/2 cups heavy (whipping) cream
2 tablespoons moist, leftover Kona espresso
    grounds
3 egg yolks
2 tablespoons sugar
1 teaspoon unsalted butter
1/2 ounce milk chocolate

### Thai Crème Brûlée

1-1/2 cups heavy (whipping) cream
1 lemongrass stalk, white part only, split length-
    wise
One 2-inch piece fresh ginger, peeled and cut
    in 1/8-inch slices
6 Kaffir lime leaves, minced
1 Hawaiian or Thai chili, halved and seeded
3 egg yolks
2 tablespoons sugar
1 teaspoon unsalted butter

### Mango Crème Brûlée

1-1/2 cups heavy (whipping) cream
1/4 cup sliced mango, puréed
1 teaspoon fresh lemon juice
3 egg yolks
2 tablespoons sugar
1 teaspoon unsalted butter

### Liliko'i Crème Brûlée

1-1/2 cups heavy (whipping) cream
1/4 cup liliko'i pulp with seeds, or passion fruit
    juice or purée
3 egg yolks
2 tablespoons sugar
1 teaspoon unsalted butter

### Hawaiian Vintage Chocolate Crème Brûlée

1-1/2 cups heavy (whipping) cream
2 ounces Hawaiian vintage or other good-quality
    bittersweet chocolate
3 egg yolks
2 tablespoons sugar
1 teaspoon unsalted butter

### Garnish

1/2 cup granulated sugar
2 ounces chocolate, shaved
8 strips crystallized ginger
24 liliko'i seeds
1/4 cup diced raw mango
8 coffee beans
8 mint sprigs

---

*To make the* ❖
*Kona mocha*
*brûlée*

In a heavy, medium pan over very low heat, bring the cream to a low simmer. Add the espresso grounds and simmer for 5 minutes. Remove from heat and strain through 2 layers of cheesecloth into a small bowl, pressing down on the espresso with the back of a spoon to extract all the flavor.

In a double boiler over simmering water, whisk yolks and sugar together and cook until very thick, about 5 minutes. Place the pan in a bowl of ice water, gently stirring the egg mixture. Stir in the infused cream, butter, and milk chocolate until the chocolate is melted and the mixture is blended.

Remove from the ice bath, place in a small bowl, cover, and refrigerate.

*To make the* ❖
*Thai brûlée*

In a heavy, medium pan over very low heat, bring the cream to a low simmer. Add the lemongrass, ginger, lime leaves, and chili. Simmer for 15 minutes. Remove from heat and strain through 2 layers of cheesecloth into a small bowl, pressing down on the flavorings with the back of a spoon to extract all the liquid.

In a double boiler over simmering water, whisk yolks and sugar together and cook until very thick, about 5 minutes. Place the pan in

*continued on the next page*

a bowl of ice water, gently stirring the egg mixture. Stir in the infused cream and butter until blended.

Remove from the ice bath, place in a small bowl, cover, and refrigerate.

To make the ❖
mango brûlée

In a heavy, medium pan over very low heat, bring the cream to a low simmer. Add the mango puree and lemon juice and simmer for 8 to 10 minutes. Remove from heat and strain through 2 layers of cheesecloth into a small bowl, pressing down on the pulp with the back of a spoon to extract all the liquid.

In a double boiler over simmering water, whisk yolks and sugar together and cook until very thick, about 5 minutes. Place the pan in a bowl of ice water, gently stirring the egg mixture. Stir in the infused cream and butter until blended.

Remove from the ice bath, place in a small bowl, cover, and refrigerate.

To make the ❖
liliko'i brûlée

In a heavy, medium pan over very low heat, bring the cream to a low simmer. Add the liliko'i pulp and seeds, juice, or puree and simmer for 8 to 10 minutes. Remove from heat and strain through 2 layers of cheesecloth into a small bowl, pressing down on the pulp with the back of a spoon to extract all the liquid.

In a double boiler over simmering water, whisk yolks and sugar together and cook until very thick, about 5 minutes. Place the pan in a bowl of ice water, gently stirring the egg mixture. Stir in the infused cream and butter until blended.

Remove from the ice bath, place in a small bowl, cover, and refrigerate.

To make the ❖
chocolate brûlée

In a heavy, medium pan over very low heat, bring the cream to a low simmer. Remove from heat and stir in the chocolate. In the top of a double boiler over simmering water, whisk together the egg yolks and sugar and cook together until very thick, about 5 minutes. Place the pan in a bowl of ice water, gently stirring the mixture. Stir in the chocolate mixture and butter. Remove from the ice bath, place in a small bowl, cover, and refrigerate.

To serve ❖

Preheat the broiler. Spoon each flavor of brûlée into 8 individual ceramic Chinese soup spoons. Sprinkle 1/2 teaspoon sugar over each. Place under the broiler for 2 or 4 seconds, or until glazed. Top each flavor with the appropriate garnish: a coffee bean on the Kona mocha, crystallized ginger on the Thai, the reserved liliko'i seeds on the liliko'i, diced mango on the mango, and chocolate shavings on the chocolate. Arrange 5 spoons, one of each flavor, side by side on a long rectangular plate and garnish the plate with mint. Repeat with remaining spoons.

*Five Spoons of Crème Brûlée*

**Serves 4**

Hawai'i knows how to make the most of sweet potatoes, combining two different colors for these sautéed cakes. Pineapple and coconut add more tropical tastes. Start the ice cream at least two days ahead.

**Mark Hetzel**

Four Seasons
Resort Maui
Wailea, Maui

### Pineapple Ice Cream
3/4 cup diced dried pineapple
3 tablespoons Japanese bourbon or other
    good bourbon
3 tablespoons water
1-1/2 cups heavy (whipping) cream
3-1/2 cups pineapple juice
1/2 vanilla bean, halved lengthwise
Four 1-inch pieces ginger, peeled and sliced
9 egg yolks
1/2 cup granulated sugar
2/3 cup simple syrup (page 159)

### Coconut Crème Fraîche
2-1/2 cups heavy (whipping) cream
1-1/2 cups (12 ounces) coconut milk
2 tablespoons buttermilk

### Sweet Potato Cake
1 sweet potato
1 Okinawan sweet potato
1/4 cup Maui natural sugar or other raw sugar
2 eggs
1/2 vanilla bean, halved lengthwise
2 tablespoons all-purpose flour
1/2 teaspoon ground cinnamon
4 tablespoons clarified butter (page 140)
4 strips Candied Ginger (recipe follows)

To make the ❖
ice cream

In a medium bowl, stir together the dried pineapple, bourbon, and water (if using a bourbon other than Japanese bourbon, dilute it by adding 1 tablespoon water). Cover and refrigerate overnight.

The next day, put the pineapple in a fine-meshed sieve over a bowl to drain. In a heavy medium saucepan, bring the cream, 1-1/2 cups of the pineapple juice, the vanilla bean, and ginger to a boil over medium-high heat. Set aside. In a small bowl, whisk together the yolks and sugar until pale in color. Stir a large spoonful of the hot cream mixture into the egg yolks, and then add the egg mixture to the pan. Stirring constantly, cook over medium heat for 1-1/2 minutes, or until the mixture thickens and coats the spoon. Strain through a fine-meshed sieve into a medium bowl. Cover and refrigerate overnight.

Whisk the remaining 2 cups pineapple juice and the simple syrup into the chilled custard. Freeze in an ice cream maker according to the manufacturer's instructions. When the ice cream is partially frozen but still can be stirred, fold in all but 1/2 cup of the soaked dried pineapple and return to the freezer. Reserve the 1/2 cup pineapple for garnish.

To make the ❖ crème fraiche

In a medium bowl, blend all the ingredients together and let sit in a warm place (85°F to 90°F) overnight.

To make the ❖ cake

Grate the sweet potatoes with the coarse holes of a grater or grate in a food processor. Rinse quickly in cold water. In a medium bowl, stir the sugar and eggs together. Scrape the seeds from the vanilla bean into the flour (discard the pod). Add the flour and cinnamon to the eggs and stir to make a smooth batter. Stir in the grated sweet potatoes.

In a medium sauté pan or skillet, melt the butter over medium-high heat. Place a 3-by-1/2-inch ring mold in the pan. Spoon 1/4 cup of the sweet potato batter into the ring, pressing it together and smoothing the top. Cook for 1-1/2 minutes, or until a light golden crust forms. With a metal spatula, turn the mold, running a knife around the inside of the ring after turning. Cook for 1-1/2 minutes, or until golden on the second side. Using the spatula, remove the pancake in the mold and drain on a paper towel. Remove the mold. Repeat to make 4 pancakes.

To serve ❖

Place each pancake on a dessert plate and dust with confectioners' sugar. Place 2 large tablespoons of coconut crème fraîche beside each cake. Add a scoop of ice cream to each. Scatter the reserved pineapple pieces in 3 small groups of 4 to 5 pieces on each plate, and stand a strip of candied ginger to one side of the cake.

*continued on the next page*

# Candied Ginger

Makes 1 cup

10 inches fresh ginger, peeled and cut in julienne
1/2 cup sugar
1/4 cup water
1 tablespoon corn syrup
Granulated sugar for dusting

In a heavy, medium saucepan, cover the ginger with water and bring to a boil. Drain, leaving the ginger in the pan. In another heavy, medium saucepan, combine the sugar, water, and corn syrup and bring to a boil over medium-high heat, stirring constantly. Cook for 2 minutes, then pour the mixture over the ginger. Cook the ginger and sugar mixture over low heat for 1 hour. Cover and let stand overnight.

Bring the mixture to a boil, reduce heat to low, and simmer 1 hour. Place a wire rack over a baking pan lined with parchment paper or aluminum foil. Lift the ginger out of the syrup with tongs and place on the rack to dry completely. Roll in granulated sugar and store in an airtight container for up to 1 month.

*Hawaiian Sweet Potato Cakes with Pineapple Ice Cream and Coconut Crème Fraîche*

Serves 8

This dense cake can be baked a day ahead and finished on the day you plan to serve it. The chocolate, coffee, and macadamia nuts bring the Big Island to mind.

**Gerard Reversade**

Gerard's at the
Plantation Inn
Lāhainā, Maui

5 ounces bittersweet chocolate
1 cup macadamia nuts
3/4 cup granulated sugar
8 eggs, separated
1 cup unsalted butter at
    room temperature
Pinch of salt

**Coating and Garnish**
1-1/2 cups heavy (whipping) cream
4 ounces bittersweet chocolate
2/3 cup (3 ounces) macadamia nuts, chopped
    and toasted (page 151)
1 tablespoon coffee extract
1 tablespoon Kahlúa or other coffee-flavored
    liqueur
8 fresh strawberries, hulled

Preheat the oven to 375°F. Place a round of parchment or waxed paper in the bottom of an 8-inch round cake pan or springform pan, and tie a collar of parchment or waxed paper around the sides to extend 2 inches over the top of the pan. Butter and flour the paper. Soften the chocolate by leaving it in a warm place for 10 minutes. Put the nuts and sugar in a blender or food processor and pulverize the nuts.

In a double boiler, beat the egg yolks until very pale in color. Place over barely simmering water to warm. Melt the chocolate in a double boiler over simmering water. Stir in the butter until blended. With a wire whisk, gently stir the chocolate into the yolks. With the same whisk, stir in the nut mixture until the sugar has melted.

In a large bowl, beat the egg whites with the salt until they form stiff peaks. Stir 1/2 cup of the egg whites into the chocolate mixture to lighten it; then gently fold all of the egg whites into the chocolate mixture. Transfer the batter to the prepared cake pan. Bake for 45 minutes, or until a toothpick inserted in the center comes out clean. Let cool in the pan until just warm to the touch, then invert onto a wire rack and let cool completely to room temperature. The cake will deflate slightly as it cools. It can be covered and set aside overnight at this point.

To make the ❖
coating and
garnish

In a heavy, medium saucepan, warm 1 cup of the cream over medium heat and stir the chocolate into the cream until completely melted. Place the cake on a wire rack over a baking sheet and pour the chocolate mixture over the cake, completely coating the top and sides. Smooth with a spatula. Let cool to firm slightly, then press the chopped macadamia nuts into the chocolate. Using a broad spatula, transfer the cake to a plate.

In a deep bowl, beat the remaining 1/2 cup cream until soft peaks begin to form. Beat in the coffee extract and Kahlúa until stiff peaks form. Put the cream in a pastry bag fitted with a large star tip and pipe rosettes on and around the cake. Garnish with strawberries.

*Flourless Macadamia Nut-Chocolate Cake*

Serves 4

This is a dessert to share with others. One large dish is prepared and presented at the table with dessert spoons and forks for everyone. If you prefer, you may divide the ingredients among individual plates.

**Mark Ellman**

Maui Tacos
Lāhainā, Maui

### Caramel Sauce
1 cup plus 6 tablespoons sugar
2/3 cup water
1 teaspoon cream of tartar
1 cup heavy (whipping) cream
1 teaspoon butter
4 ounces Hawaiian vintage or other fine-quality bittersweet chocolate, broken into small pieces

### Fruit
Select 11 fruits from the following fruits, or a total of 2-3/4 cups of any combination:
1/4 cup sliced star fruit
1/4 cup sliced peeled kiwi fruit
3 coquitos, or 1/4 cup grated fresh coconut
1/4 cup sliced peeled mango
1/4 cup sliced peeled papaya
1/4 cup sliced peeled lychees
1/4 cup sliced peeled apple banana or regular banana
1/4 cup sliced fresh strawberries
1/4 cup fresh or frozen blueberries
1/4 cup fresh raspberries
1/4 cup fresh blackberries
1/4 cup fresh marionberries or boysenberries
1/4 cup cubed Maui or other pineapple
2 scoops Macadamia Nut Ice Cream (page 150)

To make the ❖
sauce

In a heavy saucepan, combine the sugar, water, and cream of tartar and cook over high heat until coppery brown. Remove from heat and whisk in the cream, continuing to whisk until the mixture has cooled to room temperature. Whisk in the butter. Set aside.

To serve ❖

Preheat the broiler. On a large ovenproof shallow bowl, drizzle the caramel sauce in a lacy design. Sprinkle the chocolate pieces over the caramel and spoon the fruit over the caramel and chocolate. Place the plate under the broiler for 3 to 5 minutes, or until the fruit is heated. Mound the ice cream in the center and serve immediately.

Caramel Miranda

# Sam Choy's Pineapple Cheesecake

Makes one 9-inch
cheesecake,
serves 8

Pineapple flavors the rich filling and dresses the plates in this island version of cheesecake. The simple candylike crust features macadamia nuts, another island touch.

**Robert Eng**

Chef Mavro's
Honolulu, Oʻahu

### Macadamia Nut Crust
1 cup macadamia nuts
1/2 cup sugar
3 tablespoons unsalted butter, melted

### Filling
1-3/4 pounds cream cheese at room temperature
1 cup sugar
1 teaspoon grated orange zest
1 teaspoon grated lemon zest
4 large eggs
1-1/4 cups sour cream
5 tablespoons heavy (whipping) cream
1 pineapple, peeled, cored, and finely diced

### Midori Syrup
1 cup Midori liqueur
1/4 cup sugar

### Garnish
1 cup crème anglaise (page 146)
1/2 cup heavy (whipping) cream, whipped to
    stiff peaks
8 fresh mint sprigs

To make the ❖
crust

Preheat the oven to 375°F. Line the bottom of an 8-inch springform or cake pan with a circle of parchment paper or aluminum foil. In a blender or food processor, grind the nuts to the texture of coarse meal. Add the sugar and blend. Add the melted butter gradually and blend until all the nut-sugar mixture is moistened. With your fingers, press the mixture evenly into bottom of the prepared pan to create a 1/4-inch-thick crust. Bake the crust for 5 minutes, or until lightly browned. Let cool.

*continued on the next page*

**To make the filling** ❖ Reduce the oven temperature to 350°F. In a food processor or an electric mixer on slow speed, cream the cheese, sugar, and zests together until fluffy. Scrape the bowl and beaters with a rubber spatula at each stage of preparation. Add the eggs one at a time, beating thoroughly after each addition. Mix in the sour cream. Add the heavy cream and mix thoroughly. Pour half of the batter into the cooled crust in the pan.

Place the pineapple in a towel, roll up the towel, and wring as much juice as possible out of the pineapple pieces. Sprinkle about 1/2 cup pineapple evenly over the filling, avoiding the center and outside edge of the batter. Reserve the remaining pineapple for garnish. Pour in the rest of the filling to within 1/8 inch of the top. Press down any pineapple that has floated to the surface so that it does not burn. Set the filled pan in a deeper pan and fill the outer pan halfway up the cake pan with hot water. Place in the oven and bake for 60 to 75 minutes, or until a knife inserted in the center comes out clean.

**To make the syrup** ❖ In a heavy, small saucepan over medium-high heat, blend the Midori and sugar. Bring to a boil, lower heat to medium, and cook until reduced to a thick syrup, 5 to 7 minutes.

**To serve** ❖ Place 2 tablespoons of crème anglaise on each dessert plate and spread to cover the plate. Unmold the cheesecake and cut into 8 slices, dipping the knife into hot water to clean it between each cut. Center a slice on each plate. Place the whipped cream in a pastry bag fitted with a medium star tip and pipe a rosette of cream onto the wide portion of each slice. Garnish with a mint leaf. Place 2 tablespoons of reserved chopped pineapple next to each slice. Place the Midori syrup in a squeeze bottle and squeeze in small loops around the plate in the crème anglaise. With the point of a sharp knife, pull through the syrup to form a pleasing design.

Sam Choy's Pineapple Cheesecake

# Honey and Hawaiian Vintage Chocolate Ganache with Gold-dusted Chocolate Leaves and Poha Berry Sauce

**Serves 4**

A rich-as-Croesus dessert combines the melting texture and taste of honey ganache with bittersweet chocolate frills garnished with gold leaf. The slightly tart sauce provides counterpoint to the richness of the chocolate. It can, of course, be made without the touch of gold; sprinkle just a little confectioners' sugar on each frill if you prefer.

**Philippe Padovani**

Padovani's Restaurant and Wine Bar at the DoubleTree Alana Waikīkī, Oʻahu

### Kiawe Honey Ganache
1/4 cup heavy (whipping) cream
1/2 Polynesian or other vanilla bean, halved
   lengthwise
2 tablespoons Kiawe or other fragrant honey
2 ounces Hawaiian vintage or other fine-quality
   bittersweet chocolate, chopped
2 tablespoons unsalted butter

### Poha Berry Sauce
1 cup milk
1/2 Polynesian or other vanilla bean, split
   lengthwise
3 egg yolks
1/4 cup sugar
1 cup fresh poha berries or Cape
   Gooseberries or raspberries

### Chocolate Leaves
9 ounces Hawaiian vintage or other high-quality
   bittersweet chocolate
2 tablespoons canola or other light vegetable oil
2 sheets gold leaf (optional), or confectioners'
   sugar for dusting

To make the ❖ ganache

In a heavy saucepan, bring the cream to a boil over medium-high heat. Add the vanilla bean and honey. Set aside for 15 minutes to infuse the flavors. Remove the vanilla bean and add the chocolate, stirring until the chocolate has melted and the ganache is smooth. Pour into a small bowl and stir in the butter. Set aside and let cool.

**To make the sauce** ✧ In a medium saucepan, bring the milk to a boil over medium-high heat and add the vanilla bean. Set aside for 15 minutes to infuse the flavors. Remove the vanilla bean. In a medium bowl, combine the egg yolks and sugar and whisk until smooth. Pour the hot milk over the mixture, stirring constantly. Pour the egg mixture into the pan and cook over medium heat, stirring constantly, until the sauce is thick enough to coat the spoon. Be careful not to let it boil. Place the berries in a medium bowl and strain the sauce through a fine-meshed sieve into the bowl over the berries. With a mixer, blend until smooth. Place the bowl in a bowl of ice water to chill the sauce quickly. Cover and refrigerate.

**To make the chocolate leaves** ✧ In a double boiler over simmering water, melt the chocolate and heat to 100°F. Add the oil to the chocolate and blend well.

Let cool to 90°F. Using 2 ungreased jelly roll pans, pour half of the melted chocolate evenly over the surface of each pan, spread it out, and let cool completely. With a spatula, putty knife, or your thumbnail, scrape the chocolate off the pan in 1-1/2-inch frilled strips and pinch the loose pieces at one end for a leaflike design. Make 6 leaves for each plate. Using the point of a knife, with very light strokes, brush off the gold from the back of half of a gold sheet until the gold attaches to the chocolate. Set aside.

**To serve** ✧ Use 4 chilled dessert plates. Fill a pastry bag with the ganache and pipe 5 dots about 1 inch in diameter near the edge of each plate. Attach 1 leaf per dot in a pleasing pattern. If using confectioners' sugar instead of gold, dust with confectioners' sugar. Divide the sauce among the plates and pour a border of sauce around each leaf pattern.

*Honey and Hawaiian Vintage Chocolate Ganache with*
*Gold-dusted Chocolate Leaves and Poha Berry Sauce*

# Black Sesame Nougatines with Green Tea Mousse and Glazed Chestnuts

These napoleon-like desserts blend the Asian tastes of black sesame seeds and green tea with the old world flavor of caramelized chestnuts. Star fruit lends a tropical look and taste, although other fruit could be used.

**Katsuo Sugiura (Chef Suki)**

The Polo Lounge at the Beverly Hills Hotel
Beverly Hills, California

### Nougatines
3/4 cup plus 2 tablespoons unsalted butter
1-1/4 cups granulated sugar
1/4 cup honey
1/3 cup heavy (whipping) cream
2 cups black sesame seeds
3/4 cup bread flour

### Green Tea Mousse
15 egg yolks
1-1/3 cups granulated sugar
2 tablespoons green tea powder
4 cups heavy (whipping) cream
2 tablespoons Grand Marnier
8 egg whites
36 Glazed Chestnuts in Caramel Sauce (recipe follows)
Confectioner's sugar for dusting
3 star fruits, cut into 1/8-inch slices
1/2 cup raspberry purée (page 148)
48 fresh raspberries
8 fresh mint sprigs

---

To make the ❖ nougatines

Line a baking sheet with aluminum foil, or spray with vegetable-oil spray. In a heavy saucepan, combine the butter, sugar, honey, and cream and bring to a strong boil over medium-high heat, stirring constantly. Cook until the mixture reaches 240°F, or until a small amount dropped into a glass of cold water forms a soft, pliable ball. In a small bowl, mix together the sesame seeds and flour, then stir it into the sugar mixture and mix well. Drop by heaping tablespoonfuls 3 inches apart onto the prepared baking sheet. Bake for 12 minutes, or until golden. Let cool. Makes about 38 pieces; store in an airtight container.

*continued on the next page*

In a large bowl, beat the yolks until foamy. Gradually add one cup of the sugar, beating continually, until fluffy. Beat the green tea powder into the egg mixture until thoroughly blended. Stir in the cream and Grand Marnier until blended. Cover and refrigerate. In a large bowl, beat the egg whites until foamy. Gradually add the remaining 1/3 cup sugar while beating until the egg whites form stiff, glossy peaks.

To assemble ❖

Lay 1 nougatine on a serving plate. Put the mousse in a large pastry bag fitted with a large plain tip and pipe a 3/4-inch-thick mound of mousse on the nougatine. Pour 1 large spoonful of caramel sauce on the mousse and press 3 glazed chestnuts into the caramel. Place another nougatine on top of the mousse. Repeat with a second layer of mousse, caramel, and 3 more chestnuts. Dust a nougatine heavily with confectioners' sugar and place on the top. Heat a metal skewer over high heat and lay it across the sugar in a criss-cross design, letting the heat melt and caramelize the sugar. Repeat with the remaining nougatines and mousse. Cut each star fruit slice in half. Garnish each plate with 3 teaspoons raspberry purée, three star fruit halves, 6 raspberries, 3 chestnuts, and a mint sprig.

■ ■ ■

# *Glazed Chestnuts in Caramel Sauce*

Makes 3 cups

36 canned chestnuts, drained
2 cups water
1 cup sugar

Pat the chestnuts dry with paper towels. In a heavy saucepan, combine the water and sugar and stir over low heat just until the sugar dissolves. Increase the heat to medium-high and continue to cook, brushing away the crystals that form on the sides of the pan with a damp brush. Do not stir. Let the mixture boil until the sugar turns golden brown. Remove from heat immediately and place the pan in a bowl of ice water. When the caramel has cooled slightly, dip the chestnuts in the caramel to coat, and set aside on aluminum foil or waxed paper. If the caramel thickens too much before use, warm it gently to melt.

*Black Sesame Nougatines with*
*Green Tea Mousse and Glazed Chestnuts*

**Serves 6**

Guiltless, silky smooth, and rich-tasting—this may be the perfect chocolate pie. The basic recipe can be garnished with different kinds of fruit and different colors of chocolate. Silken tofu is available in the Asian foods section of grocery stores; it is creamier than firm tofu. Fruitsource® is a liquid sweetener.

**Kathleen Daelemans**

Café Kula
Grand Wailea
Resort
Wailea, Maui

### Crust
10 low-fat graham crackers, broken
2 tablespoons maple syrup
2 tablespoons canola oil
2 tablespoons water

### Filling
1/2 cup Fruitsource® (available at natural foods stores), or honey
1/4 cup maple syrup or honey
21 ounces silken tofu
1 tablespoon vanilla extract
3/4 cup unsweetened cocoa powder

### Garnish
3/4 cup raspberry purée (page 148)
1/2 cup banana slices
18 fresh raspberries
6 fresh mint sprigs
Unsweetened cocoa powder for dusting
6 tablespoons grated white chocolate

---

**To make the crust** ❖ Preheat the oven to 350°F. In a food processor, grind the crackers to fine crumbs. Pour into a medium bowl, add the remaining ingredients, and mix together until it forms a mass. Or, to make by hand, combine all the ingredients in a small bowl and stir together until the mixture forms a mass. Put the dough in an 8-inch pie pan and press with your fingers to form a 1/4-inch-thick shell. Bake for 8 minutes, or until set and lightly browned. Let cool in the pan.

**To make the filling** ❖ In a medium saucepan over medium heat, combine the Fruitsource and maple syrup or honey and cook for 5 minutes. Combine this mixture and all the remaining filling ingredients in a blender or food processor and blend until smooth. Pour the mixture into the cooled pie crust. Refrigerate for at least 2 hours, or until firm but pudding-like.

**To serve** ❖ Cut the pie and place slices on individual dessert plates. Sprinkle 2 tablespoons of raspberry purée on each plate and garnish with a few banana slices, 3 fresh raspberries, and a mint leaf. Sprinkle the rim of the plate with cocoa powder, and sprinkle 1 tablespoon white chocolate over the pie.

---

Bittersweet Chocolate Pie

Serves 4

This beautiful torte of chocolate cake, hazelnut meringue, and flavored fillings is unforgettable, both for its taste and its presentation. The torte could be served by itself, of course. But try the adventure of creating the dramatic chocolate petals and wings; the reward is a piece of art.

**Gale E.
O'Malley**

Hilton Hawaiian
Village
Honolulu, O'ahu

### Chocolate Garnishes
8 ounces bittersweet chocolate
8 striped chocolate wings (page 144)
4 dark chocolate wings (page 144)
Eight 4-1/2-inch dark chocolate discs (page 144)
24 striped chocolate tulip petals (page 144)

### Hazelnut Meringues
6 egg whites
1/2 teaspoon cream of tartar
1-1/2 cups confectioners' sugar, sifted
1 cup hazelnuts, finely ground

### Chocolate Cake
4 eggs
2/3 cup sugar
1/4 cup cocoa
Pinch of salt
3/4 cup sifted cake flour
3 tablespoons unsalted butter, melted

### White Cake
4 eggs
2/3 cup sugar
2 teaspoons vanilla
Pinch of salt
1 cup sifted cake flour
3 tablespoons unsalted butter, melted

### Chocolate Buttercream
3 ounces bittersweet chocolate, chopped
2 egg yolks
1/3 cup granulated sugar
1/4 cup water
1/2 cup (1 stick) unsalted butter at room
    temperature

1/4 cup raspberry jam
36 fresh raspberries
1-1/2 cups ganache (page 142)
1/4 cup Chambord or other raspberry liqueur
1 cup heavy (whipping) cream, whipped to
    soft peaks
1 tablespoon unsweetened cocoa powder
1/2 pound marzipan
2 ounces bittersweet chocolate, melted
1 tablespoon unsweetened cocoa powder
4 lattice dark chocolate leaves (page 145)

To assemble ❖
the chocolate
garnishes

(To assemble
the wings)

Line a sheet pan with waxed paper. In the top of a double boiler over simmering water, melt 4 ounces of dark chocolate. Lay four striped chocolate wings, stripe-side up, on the waxed paper. Place the melted chocolate in a pastry bag or paper cone with a fine tip and pipe a quarter-sized dot of hot chocolate on the lower fourth of each wing. Press a plain chocolate wing onto each dot and hold if necessary until the chocolate sets enough to hold the wing.

Pipe another quarter-sized dot of hot chocolate onto the lower fourth of the plain wings, and press another striped wing onto each. Place in the refrigerator to set, 5 to 7 minutes.

Line another sheet pan with waxed paper. Place four discs on the waxed paper. Pipe a 2-inch dot of hot chocolate on a circle, mounding the dot. Place an assembled wing upright on the dot of chocolate and hold until it sets. Pipe additional hot chocolate at the base of the wing to secure it firmly. Place in the freezer. Repeat with the other wings. The wings can remain in the freezer for 2 days.

(To assemble
the tulip cups)

Line a sheet pan with waxed paper. In the top of a double boiler over simmering water or in a microwave, melt 4 ounces of dark chocolate. Place four discs on the waxed paper. Place the melted chocolate in a pastry bag or paper cone with a fine tip and pipe a 1-inch strip of chocolate on the rim of the disc. With the tips of your fingers lift a striped tulip petal and place it, striped-side in and point-side up, into the chocolate. Adjust with a slight outward lean and hold gently

*continued on the next page*

until it sets firmly enough to stay. Repeat with five more tulip petals. Place in the freezer. Repeat with the remaining three discs. The cups can remain in the freezer for 2 days.

To make the ❖
meringues

Preheat the oven to 200°F. Line a baking pan with parchment paper or heavy brown paper. Trace around a 4-inch ring mold to draw 4 circles on the paper. In a large bowl, beat the egg whites and cream of tartar together until foamy. Gradually beat in the confectioners' sugar until the meringue forms stiff peaks. Fold in the ground hazelnuts. Place the meringue in a pastry bag fitted with a medium plain tip and pipe a tight solid spiral on a circle drawn on the prepared baking sheet. Fill in the circle completely. Repeat with the remaining circles and smooth the tops slightly with a spatula or table knife. Bake for 1 to 1-1/2 hours, or until crisp but not browned. Remove the paper with the meringues and place on a wire rack to cool on the paper.

When cool, lift the meringues from the paper. With a sharp knife, trim the edges of each meringue circle to fit inside a 4-inch ring mold. Set aside at room temperature until ready to use.

To make the ❖
chocolate cake

Preheat the oven to 350°F. Line the bottoms of two 9-inch round cake pans with parchment paper. Warm a deep bowl: fill the bowl with warm water, empty it, and dry thoroughly. In the warmed bowl, beat the eggs and sugar together until the mixture thickens and a ribbon forms when a spoonful is drizzled on the surface. Fold the cocoa into the egg mixture. Gradually fold the salt and two thirds of the flour into the egg mixture. Blend a large spoonful of the mixture into the butter, then gently fold the butter and the remaining one third of the flour into the mixture. Pour into the prepared pans and bake for 10 minutes, or until a toothpick inserted in the center comes out clean. Let the pan cool for 10 minutes, then remove the cakes from the pans and cool completely on a wire rack. You will have two 1/2-inch thick cakes.

To make the ❖
white cake

Preheat the oven to 350°F. Line the bottoms of two 9-inch round cake pans with parchment paper. Warm a deep bowl: fill the bowl with warm water, empty it, and dry thoroughly. In the warmed bowl, beat the eggs and sugar together until the mixture thickens and a ribbon forms when a spoonful is drizzled on the surface. Stir the vanilla into the egg mixture. Gradually fold two thirds of the flour into the egg mixture. Blend a large spoonful of the mixture into the butter, then gently fold the butter and the remaining one third of the flour into the mixture. Pour into the prepared pans and bake for 10 minutes, or until a toothpick inserted in the center comes out clean. Let the pan cool for 10 minutes, then remove the cakes from the pans and cool completely on a wire rack. You will have two 1/2-inch thick cakes.

**To make the ❖ buttercream**

In a double boiler over barely simmering water, melt the chocolate. Strain the chocolate through a fine-meshed sieve into a small bowl and set aside to cool slightly. In a medium bowl, beat the egg yolks until light and fluffy. In a heavy, medium saucepan, stir the sugar and water together. Bring to a boil over medium heat, using a pastry brush to brush down any crystals that form on the sides of the pan. Do not stir the mixture while it is heating. Boil to 240°F, or until a small amount dropped into a glass of cold water forms a soft, pliable ball. Remove from heat. While beating the eggs yolks on medium speed, gradually pour a thin stream of the sugar mixture into the yolks. Increase the speed to high and continue pouring until all the sugar has been absorbed and the mixture has cooled. It will be light and fluffy.

In a small deep bowl, cream the butter. Add the butter 1 tablespoon at a time to the mixture, beating constantly, until the butter is incorporated. While beating, gradually pour the chocolate into the buttercream until completely blended and smooth. The buttercream will keep up to 2 months in the freezer.

**To assemble ❖**

Line a baking sheet with parchment paper or aluminum foil. Place four 4-inch ring molds on the sheet. Cut 4 strips of heavy flexible plastic 4 inches wide and 12-3/4 inches long to fit the inside of the ring molds. Place a plastic strip around the inside of each mold, letting it extend above the top.

Cut four 4-inch circles from the chocolate sponge. Trim each sponge circle to 1/2-inch thick. Spread a thin layer of raspberry jam on each sponge circle and place one in each prepared mold, jam-side up. Put the buttercream into a pastry bag fitted with a large plain tip and pipe a layer over each sponge. Press 6 of the raspberries into the buttercream of each torte. Put the ganache in a pastry bag fitted with a medium plain tip and pipe a layer of ganache over the raspberries. Reserve the remaining ganache for the final assembly.

*continued on the next page*

Place a meringue disc over each layer of ganache, pressing it down slightly. Sprinkle the meringue with Chambord. Press the juice from the remaining 12 raspberries, strain through a fine-meshed sieve, and gently fold the raspberry juice into the whipped cream. Spoon 2 to 3 tablespoons of the raspberry cream over each meringue.

Cut the white sponge into four 4-inch circles. Trim the sponge circles to 1/2-inch thick and press one on top of the whipped cream in each mold. Fold the cocoa powder into the raspberry cream and spoon 2 to 3 tablespoons over each cake. Smooth the tops with the back of a kitchen knife and place the molds in the freezer until firm, 2 to 3 hours.

Line a baking sheet with parchment or aluminum foil. Place a wire rack on the baking sheet. Roll the marzipan into a 1/8-inch-thick sheet and cut four 4-inch circles. In a double boiler over barely simmering water, warm the ganache to pouring consistency. Remove the molds from the freezer and gently warm the outsides of the molds with warm towels. Run the tip of a thin sharp knife around the inside of each mold to loosen the rings. Unmold the tortes onto the wire rack. Strip off the plastic. Press a skewer or fork into each torte and dip completely in the ganache, then place on the rack to drip. Press a marzipan disc onto the top of each torte while the ganache is still soft.

To serve ❖ Place a petal cup slightly off center on a dessert plate and carefully center a torte in the cup. Place the melted chocolate in a pastry bag fitted with a small plain tip. Pipe a small pool of melted chocolate on the plate and place a wing garnish in the melted chocolate, holding it in place until the chocolate cools and firms. Dust the top of the marzipan disc with cocoa powder. Pipe a 1/2-inch mound of ganache in the center and lean a chocolate lattice leaf against the ganache. Repeat with the remaining tortes.

*The Unforgettable Torte*

# The Traditional Lū'au Feast

■ ■ ■

*"Fish and poi, fish and poi. All I need is fish and poi . . ."*

Those words from a childhood song come immediately to mind whenever the subjects of lū'au and traditional Hawaiian food come up.

The lū'au is a feast that celebrates important events such as weddings, graduations, housewarmings, anniversaries, or a baby's first birthday. Whatever the occasion, it means lots of food, good feelings among friends and family, and often music and dance.

Today there are two kinds of lū'au: the kind given for tourists, and the kind given by locals in backyards, church halls, and community centers.

Tourist lū'au are blatantly commercial, with food that only remotely resembles real Hawaiian food. You are likely to find teriyaki steak, tossed green salad in large quantities, and almost no poi or raw seafood. Hawaiians, on the other hand, love raw black crab, 'opihi (limpets) and limu (seaweed), poke (marinated raw fish), and wana (sea urchin).

A lū'au put on for visitors usually has a stagey hula show and is often set near the sand at a beachfront resort hotel, or sometimes in the hotel's garden. There will be leis and flowers on the tables, and the event will be very pretty, if not terribly authentic.

But the real thing is all about cementing the bonds of friendship and family. A lū'au can last the entire weekend, with people arriving on Friday afternoon to begin the preparation. Aunties arrive from the Big Island with orchids and anthuriums for decoration. All the "calabash" (extended family related by marriage or affection) relatives are there to pitch in and help (and start partying before the actual event).

By early morning on the day of the event, the imu, or lū'au, pit, is dug and filled with hot rocks and ti leaves. A pig, often wrapped in chicken wire to hold it together after cooking, is lowered into the pit. Other foods—turkeys, laulau (ti leaf bundles of meat and fish), sweet potatoes, fish—are added, then everything is covered with leaves, burlap, and soil, and left to steam all day.

'Opihi and limu will have been gathered from the seaside, or purchased at great expense in a local market.

Now the preparation of the other food begins. The day proceeds with a lot of chopping, stirring, and laughter. The side dishes, such as poke, squid lū'au (squid cooked with taro tops and coconut milk), lomi lomi salmon (a salad of salted salmon, tomatoes, onions, and chili peppers), chicken long rice (a Chinese dish of chicken and bean thread noodles), and haupia or kulolo (coconut or taro puddings) are made ahead.

And there is always poi. Originally poi was made by peeling, cooking, and pounding taro roots into a paste. Today poi is purchased from regional factories, and the product is superior for its smoothness and consistency. For all the joking by tourists about its similarity to wallpaper paste, poi continues to be a favorite with locals. This healthy staple starch is the basis of the traditional Hawaiian diet.

Now the younger family members decorate the tables and the hall. Often long picnic tables are covered with rolls of paper. Family members and friends then decorate with ti leaves, lauae ferns, and flowers down the center. A fancier lū'au might have tapa or pareu-designed fabric tablecloths.

Just before the lū'au begins, flavored soda water in bottles, a square piece of coconut cake, red alae salt (coarse sea salt mixed with clay), raw onions, and other condiments are placed at each seat.

## SAM CHOY THROWS A LŪ'AU

Sam Choy was just a lad when he began helping out with his father's lū'au, the first of those native feasts given expressly for island visitors. Now Sam's son helps out with his lū'au. If you want to hold your own lū'au, invite your family and friends, and follow Sam's example.

The guests arrive in their finest mu'umu'u and aloha shirts. Children are always included and show up scrubbed clean and wearing their best jeans or shorts.

The music strikes up as the guests arrive—not tourist music, but the "cha-lang a-lang" variety that has been played by backyard bands for as long as anyone can remember. The hula dancers aren't uniformly slender and the dances aren't perfectly coordinated, but the dancers are the granddaughters, mothers, or uncles of the people in the group. They may forget some of the movements, but they know the meaning of the dance. It is a gift to their family—their 'ohana.

The party often continues on Sunday. The kālua pig is reheated on top of the stove with cabbage and onions. Other leftovers are heated up and laid out, or left on the stove for people to help themselves.

By early afternoon, everyone is headed home for the other side of the island, or for the airport to catch a late plane home to their own island. Now the lū'au-givers can collapse—and gather up their memories.

If you decide to give a lū'au yourself, remember that the food should be fresh and plentiful, the preparation shared, and the spirit open and loving.

*"Fish and poi. Fish and poi. All I need is fish and poi . . ."*

The perfect imu, or baking pit, is dug into the earth and lined with volcanic rocks or other rocks that will not split when heated to a high temperature, such as granite (slate, shale, and other sedimentary rocks won't work). A fire is built over the rocks and allowed to burn down until the rocks themselves are extremely hot. The rocks are then spread on the bottom of the pit and pulled to the sides; after the food is added the rocks will be piled on top of the food and the pit covered for slow cooking. The process is similar to that used for a New England clambake.

Ti leaves and banana leaves are prepared. The midrib can be cut away slightly on the back of the leaf so the leaf will bend more easily.

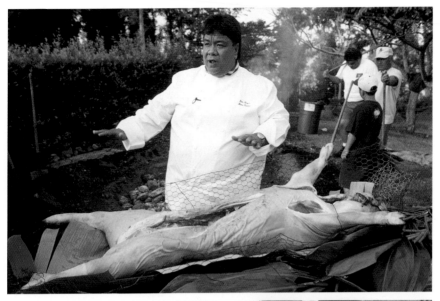

A cleaned pig is rubbed with sea salt inside and out, wrapped in banana leaves and then ti leaves, and trussed in chicken wire so it can easily be lifted from the pit when it is finished. *(Picture above)*

Hot rocks are placed in the body cavity, and the pig is lowered into the pit, covered, and slow cooked for about 6 hours. Toward the end of the cooking, other items to be baked, such as sweet potatoes, are added to the pit. *(Pictures on the right and the next page)*

The finished pig is lifted from the imu, and the meat is pulled into serving pieces. The side dishes are removed from the pit and placed on the table to be eaten. *(Picture below)*

While the pig is cooking, the tables are readied. Sam sets out dishes of other foods such as poi, several kinds of fish such as ʻōpakapaka and lomi lomi. Fresh fruit, pokes, chicken long rice, laulau, and coconut cake are all traditional. Fruit punch is the drink of choice. *(Picture on the right)*

# Lomi Lomi

Serves 12

Start the night before. Lomi lomi is very simple to make, but the salmon needs to marinate in salt water for at least 8 hours.

> 3 pounds salmon
> 1-1/2 tablespoons sea salt
> 6 tomatoes, stemmed and chopped
> 5 green onions, minced
> 2 Hawaiian or Thai chilies, minced
> 6 cups crushed ice

Debone the salmon. Chop into quarter-inch dice and sprinkle with salt. Put the salmon in a shallow baking dish filled with 4 cups of the crushed ice, cover, and refrigerate for at least 8 hours. Drain the salmon, place in a large bowl, and toss with chopped tomatoes and green onions. Toss with the remaining 2 cups crushed ice just before serving.

# Chicken Long Rice

Serves 12

The "long rice" is bean thread noodles broken into short lengths. There are as many variations of chicken long rice as there are families; don't be afraid to add your own touches.

> 8 ounces bean thread noodles, broken into 2–3-inch
>     pieces
> 4 cups chicken stock (page 155)
> 2 pounds chicken pieces, skinned, boned, and cut into
>     1-inch cubes
> One 2-inch piece of ginger, crushed
> 2 large carrots, peeled and cut into julienne
> 6 stalks celery, thinly sliced
> 1 large onion, thinly sliced
> 1 pound mushrooms, sliced

Soak the noodles in warm water to cover for 1 hour. In a soup pot, combine the chicken stock, chicken, and ginger. Bring to a boil, reduce heat to low, and simmer for 5 minutes. Add the carrots, celery, onion, and mushrooms and simmer for 4 minutes. Drain the noodles and add to the chicken mixture. Cover and cook for 5 minutes, or until the noodles are translucent.

It's all self-serve at the lū'au table. Sam Choy's son Christopher shows he knows how to carry on family tradition. (*Picture above*)

# Basic Recipes
## and Techniques

■ ■ ■

Many of the basic recipes and techniques in this chapter are classic elements of American and European cooking, such as chicken stock, and roasting and peeling bell peppers. But a variety of tropical recipes and techniques are also included. Husking coconuts, making chili pepper water, and cutting pineapple with the dexterity of a professional are some of the key steps in preparing island cuisine you'll find here.

# Brown Sauce
Makes 4 cups

This versatile Asian-style brown sauce can be used as a braising sauce for nearly any meat or vegetable. Chilled, it gels and can be used as a garnish for savories and salads.

2 tablespoons vegetable oil
2 whole green onions, finely chopped
2 tablespoons minced, peeled, fresh ginger root
4 garlic cloves, minced
1 teaspoon Sichuan peppercorns
3 star anise pods
1/2 cup beef stock (page 156)
1 cup soy sauce
1/2 cup sake
1 tablespoon sugar
1 teaspoon salt

In a large stockpot over medium-high heat, heat the oil and sauté the onions, ginger, garlic, peppercorns, and star anise until the onions are translucent and the mixture is fragrant, about 2 minutes. Add the stock, soy sauce, sake, sugar, and salt. Raise heat to high and boil for 10 to 12 minutes. Use immediately, or cover and refrigerate for up to 3 days, or freeze for up to 3 months.

# Butter

## Clarified Butter

Melt butter over low heat, then cover and refrigerate it. Once the fat has hardened, scoop it off, being careful to leave the bottom layer of milk solids. Cover the clarified butter and refrigerate for up to 2 weeks.

If you don't have time to let the butter chill, melt the butter gently so that the milk solids settle on the bottom of the pan, forming a creamy white sediment. Carefully pour off the clear yellow butter, and discard the milk solids or add them to soup or sauce.

## Herb Butter
Makes 2 cups

1/8 teaspoon garlic powder
1 teaspoon minced fresh parsley
1 teaspoon minced fresh basil
1 teaspoon minced fresh shallots
1 teaspoon minced fresh watercress
Juice of 1 lemon
1 pound (4 sticks) salted butter

In the bowl of a food processor or mixer, combine all ingredients. Beat until smooth, about 4 minutes. Pack into molds or a glass container with a lid, and refrigerate. Keeps up to 1 week.

## Citrus-Herb Butter

Makes 2 cups

Juice of 1/2 lemon
Juice of 1/2 orange
Juice of 1/2 lime
1 pound (4 sticks) salted butter
1 tablespoon dried tarragon leaves
1 tablespoon dried basil leaves
Pinch of freshly ground black pepper
1/2 teaspoon salt (optional)
1/2 teaspoon sugar (optional)

In the bowl of a food processor or mixer, combine all ingredients. Beat until smooth, about 4 minutes. Add salt and sugar to taste. Pack into molds or a glass container with a lid, and refrigerate. Keeps up to 1 week.

## Garlic Butter

Makes 2 cups

1 tablespoon garlic powder
3 minced fresh garlic cloves
Juice of 1 lemon
1 pound (4 sticks) salted butter

In the bowl of a food processor or mixer, combine all ingredients. Beat until smooth, about 4 minutes. Pack into molds or a glass container with a lid, and refrigerate. Keeps up to 1 week.

## Garlic–Herb Butter

Makes 2 cups

1 tablespoon garlic powder
1 minced fresh garlic clove
1 teaspoon minced fresh parsley
1 teaspoon minced fresh basil
1 teaspoon minced fresh shallots
1 teaspoon minced fresh watercress
Juice of 1 lemon
1 pound (4 sticks) salted butter

In the bowl of a food processor or mixer, combine all ingredients. Beat until smooth, about 4 minutes. Pack into molds or a glass container with a lid, and refrigerate. Keeps up to 1 week.

# Caramel Sauce
Makes 2 cups

This thick caramel sauce is enriched with butter and cream.

> 1-1/2 cups sugar
> 1/2 cup water
> 3 tablespoons butter
> 1 cup heavy (whipping) cream, heated
> 1/2 teaspoon vanilla extract

In a heavy, medium saucepan, combine the sugar and water and bring to a simmer over medium heat, swirling occasionally. Cover, raise the heat to medium high, and cook for 2 minutes, or until the liquid gives off large, thick bubbles. Uncover and cook, swirling the syrup, until it turns golden brown.

Remove from heat and stir in the butter with a wooden spoon. Add the cream, stirring constantly, then add the vanilla. Return the pan to low heat and stir constantly until any lumps have melted and the syrup is smooth. Serve warm over ice cream or cake, or pour into a jar, cover, and refrigerate for up to 1 week.

# Chili Oil
Makes 1 cup

In a medium bowl, combine 4 Hawaiian or Thai peppers with 1 cup of olive oil. Cover and let sit for a minimum of 48 hours. Pour through a fine-meshed sieve into a glass jar or bottle and cover.

# Chocolate

## Ganache

> 1 cup heavy (whipping) cream
> 1 pound semisweet chocolate, chopped

In a heavy pan, bring the cream to a boil over medium-high heat. Remove from heat. Add the chocolate and stir until melted. Let cool thoroughly.

## Chocolate Sauce
Makes 4 cups

> 1 cup sugar
> 2 cups half-and-half
> 8 ounces bittersweet or semisweet chocolate, chopped
> 8 ounces unsweetened chocolate, chopped

In a heavy, large saucepan, combine the sugar and half-and-half and heat over medium-low heat until hot but not boiling. Add the chocolate and stir until the chocolate is melted and the mixture is smooth. Serve warm, or pour into a jar, cover, and refrigerate for up to 1 week.

**To melt chocolate:** Melt chopped chocolate in a double boiler over barely simmering water. Stir until smooth.

**To pipe chocolate:** Place melted chocolate in a small pastry bag fitted with a very fine tip. Use as you would any piping. For larger lines, put the chocolate in a squeeze bottle. For small amounts of melted chocolate for piping narrow lines or small dots to affix other decorations, place the chocolate in a small zip-top plastic bag. Melt the chocolate in the bag in a double boiler over barely simmering water. When the chocolate has liquified, snip a tiny opening in one corner of the plastic bag and use the bag as your "pastry bag" for piping.

**To temper chocolate:** Tempering is used to prepare chocolate for coating and molding. Heating and then cooling the chocolate to precise temperatures makes the chocolate shiny. In the top of a double boiler over not-quite-simmering water, melt chopped chocolate and heat to 100°F. Do not let any water come in contact with the chocolate. Remove the pan from the hot water bath, let cool to 90°F. Set the pan on a heating pad set on low to maintain the temperature at 90°F.

## Chocolate Garnishes

Hawaiian Vintage Chocolate is the only chocolate grown in the United States. Hawaiian chefs frequently use beautiful chocolate garnishes to complete masterpiece desserts. Chocolate can be very tricky, "seizing" (stiffening) instantly if a drop of water accidentally falls into the pan, "breaking" (separating) if heat is applied incorrectly, and requiring a "tempering" process for coating and molding work. Yet sculpted flowers, leaves, geometric pieces and filigree designs are worth the effort of learning to work with this tempermental ingredient.

The recipe which follows gives steps for forming garnishes used with desserts in this book, and the quantity will make at least enough of any one type to garnish four dessert plates. At any time while you are working chocolate, you can warm it just slightly with a heat lamp or blow dryer to keep it flexible. Any excess chocolate at any step can be scraped back into the pan and allowed to remelt. Chocolate garnishes can be held in the refrigerator or freezer until ready to use.

**To make chocolate curls:** Melt 2 ounces chopped bittersweet chocolate in a double boiler and heat to 100°F. Let cool to 90°F. Pour the chocolate out on a baking sheet and spread it into a smooth layer 1/8-inch thick. When cool, scrape up narrow strips of chocolate with the back of your nail or a narrow spatula, creating small curls.

**To make flat chocolate shapes:** Place a heavy flexible plastic sheet on a work surface. Melt chopped bittersweet chocolate in a double boiler and heat to 100°F. Let cool to 90°F. Pour the chocolate out on the plastic and spread it out into a smooth layer of the desired thickness, usually just over 1/8 inch thick. Let cool to room temperature and use molds, cookie cutters, or the tip of a sharp knife to cut out the desired shapes. Pull the excess chocolate from around the shapes and place the designs in the refrigerator to set.

**To make plain chocolate wings:** Melt 4 ounces of bittersweet chocolate and spread out as described above. Cut into 4 free-form wing shapes when cooled.

**To make chocolate discs:** Melt 4 ounces of bittersweet chocolate and spread out as described above. Cut into eight 4-inch discs when cooled.

## Striped Chocolate
Makes one 12-by-16-inch sheet

This recipe makes dark chocolate striped with white chocolate. To create dark lines on a white background, simply use the dark chocolate first. Striped chocolate is used in the Unforgettable Torte (page 122).

>    4 ounces white chocolate, chopped
>    8 ounces bittersweet chocolate, chopped

You will need a sheet of heavy flexible plastic, a long thin spatula, and a masonry comb. Melt chopped white chocolate in a double boiler and heat to 100°F. Let cool to 90°F. Pour the white chocolate out onto the plastic. With the spatula, spread the chocolate out to a thin layer of less than 1/8 inch. Using the masonry comb, scrape through the chocolate down to the plastic to create straight lines in the chocolate. Refrigerate for about 5 minutes, or until set.

Melt chopped bittersweet chocolate in a double boiler and heat to 100°F. Let cool to 90°F. Remove the white chocolate lines from the refrigerator. With a clean spatula, spread the dark chocolate over the back of the stripes. Be careful not to disturb the stripes. Refrigerate for 5 minutes.

**Striped chocolate wings:** After the chocolate has set slightly, cut through the chocolate and plastic with a sharp knife and drape it across a curved surface, plastic-side down. Refrigerate until set. Peel away the plastic to expose the shiny striped surface. Makes 8 wings.

**Striped chocolate tulip petals:** Let the chocolate set at room temperature and use a cookie cutter to stamp out the desired shapes. Pull the excess chocolate from around the cut shapes. Put the shapes, still on the plastic, in the refrigerator to firm completely, and peel the plastic from the designs. Makes 24 chocolate tulip petals.

An alternative method of making striped chocolate is to pour and smooth a thin layer of chocolate, then pipe stripes of the same color or contrasting color chocolate on top of the smooth layer.

**Dark Chocolate Lattice Leaves:** Place a heavy flexible plastic sheet on a work surface. Melt 2 ounces chopped bittersweet chocolate in a double boiler and heat to 100°F. Let cool to 90°F. Drizzle the chocolate onto the plastic in a thin stream from the tip of a spoon, crisscrossing the strands of chocolate. When set, cut the lattice into leaf shapes and dust with cocoa powder.

**Chocolate filigree:** Draw a design to follow. Lay the design on the work surface and place a sheet of heavy flexible clear plastic on top of it. Melt 2 ounces chopped bittersweet chocolate in a double boiler and heat to 100°F. Let cool to 90°F. Place the melted chocolate in a pastry bag fitted with a fine writing tip and pipe the chocolate over the design, following the lines. Lift the plastic and place it on a flat sheet pan or, if a curved design is desired, lay it across a curved surface. Refrigerate to set.

# Coconuts

**Shelling a Coconut:** Puncture one of the "eyes" of a husked coconut with an icepick. Pour out the coconut water, reserving it if desired, then crack the coconut by hitting it with a heavy hammer in the middle where the shell is the widest. Continue rapping around the coconut until you have cracked the shell in a circle and can separate the two halves. Pry the coconut meat out of the shell with a sharp, heavy knife. Or, heat the coconut in a preheated 350°F oven for 15 minutes, remove, and let cool. Wrap the coconut in a kitchen towel and crack into pieces with a hammer.

**Grating Fresh Coconut Meat:** Break the shelled fresh meat into small pieces. With a sharp, heavy knife, peel off the brown outer skin. Grate the meat with the large holes of a grater or with a vegetable peeler. Coconut can also be grated in a food processor with the shredding disc, or chopped finely with the steel blade.

**Toasting Coconut:** Preheat the oven to 350°F. Cut the peeled coconut meat into thin strips with a sharp paring knife. Spread the coconut strips in a single layer on a baking sheet and toast in the oven for 15 to 20 minutes, until golden. If the coconut has been dried already, reduce the toasting time to 5 to 7 minutes.

**Making Coconut Milk:** Place the freshly grated coconut meat from 1 coconut in a square of cheesecloth. Bring the edges of the cheesecloth together and tie with a piece of string. Place the cheesecloth bundle in a large pot. Bring enough water to cover the bundle to a boil in a separate pot, and pour over the coconut bundle. Let cool. When the water and coconut are cool enough to handle, with your hands, squeeze the

coconut milk out through the cheesecloth into the pot. Use immediately or refrigerate for up to 2 days.

## Cream Puffs
Makes about 15 2-inch puffs

> 1/2 cup milk
> 1/2 cup water
> 1/2 cup (1 stick) unsalted butter
> 1 cup unbleached all-purpose flour
> 2 tablespoons sugar
> 4 eggs

Preheat oven to 400°F. Line 2 baking sheets with parchment paper or grease them. In a medium saucepan, combine the milk, water, and butter and bring to a boil over medium-high heat. Add the flour and sugar all at once and stir the mixture until it forms a ball and comes away from the side of the pan, about 2 or 3 minutes. Add the eggs one at a time, stirring until each is blended. Remove from heat and let stand for 5 minutes.

Place the mixture in a pastry bag fitted with a 1-inch plain tip. Pipe 1-1/2-inch-diameter portions 2 inches apart on the prepared pans. Bake for 10 minutes, then reduce heat to 350°F and bake for 10 to 15 minutes, or until light brown.

## Crème Anglaise
Makes 2 cups

> 4 egg yolks
> 1/3 cup sugar
> 1-1/2 cups milk, heated
> 1 vanilla bean, halved lengthwise, or
>     2 teaspoons vanilla extract
> 1 tablespoon unsalted butter at room temperature
>     (optional)

In a heavy, medium saucepan, whisk the egg yolks over low heat until they are pale in color. Whisk in the sugar 1 tablespoon at a time, then whisk until the mixture reaches the consistency of cake batter.

Whisk in the milk and vanilla bean, if using, then stir continuously with a wooden spoon until the custard coats the spoon and a line drawn down the back of the spoon remains visible. Remove from heat and stir in the vanilla extract. Strain through a fine-meshed sieve. If the custard is to be chilled, press a sheet of plastic wrap directly onto the surface to prevent a skin from forming, or dot the top with bits of butter. Chill the custard for up to 2 days.

*Note: If the custard begins to overheat and the egg yolks are forming lumps, remove it immediately from the heat and whisk briskly to cool the mixture. Push the custard through a fine-meshed sieve with the back of a spoon to remove the lumps. If it has not sufficiently thickened, return it to heat to complete cooking.*

## Croutons

Preheat the oven to 300°F. Cut the crusts from 5 or 6 slices of day-old or leftover bread. Slice the bread into 1/2-inch dice. In a sauté pan or skillet over high heat, melt 2 tablespoons of butter and 2 tablespoons of olive oil. Add the bread cubes and stir until coated on all sides. Spread the cubes over the prepared sheet pan in a single layer and bake until crisp and light brown in color. Cool; store in a sealed container up to 2 days, or in the freezer. To make garlic or herb croutons, use one of the flavored butters, pages 140-141, and proceed as directed.

**To "French" a lamb chop:** Hold a rack of lamb so that the bones extend away from you. Using a sharp knife, scrape and cut away the meat from the bones. Press the chop meat back toward the chops between each bone, leaving the bones clean. Butchers will usually perform this task for you.

## Fruit

**Liliko'i (Passion Fruit):** To use, cut the fruit in half and peel. For juice, press the fruit through a sieve and discard the pulp.

**Mango:** Lay the mango on its flattest side on a cutting board. With a small, sharp knife, cut a thick slice off the top, avoiding the stone. Flip the fruit over and repeat the process on the other side. Cut away any flesh still clinging to the stone and discard the pit. Score the flesh inside the large halves, and, using your fingers, bend the skin backwards until it is almost inside out, which spreads the chunks apart. Cut them away from the skin and proceed to puree or use as desired.

**Papaya:** With a sharp knife, remove the skin, scoop out the seeds, and slice the meat. Many chefs reserve a few of the seeds, wash them, and use them as a garnish. Papaya contains an enzyme that breaks down protein; rinse and add papaya as close to serving time as possible when using in dishes containing gelatin.

**Pineapple:** Protect your hands with a small towel and twist or cut the top off a fresh pineapple. With a small sharp knife, cut the stem and bottom ends off the fruit. Stand the fruit upright on a cutting board and use the knife to slice off the tough, prickly outer peel from top to bottom. When the yellow core is exposed, cut out and discard any "eyes" left. The eyes lie in spirals around the fruit; making a V-shaped

cut along the spiral line will quickly remove a whole row of eyes. Repeat until all eyes are removed. Fresh pineapple contains an enzyme which will break down protein; rinse well and add as close to serving time as possible when using in dishes containing gelatin.

**Sapote:** With a sharp knife, peel the skin from the fruit and cut the flesh into pieces.

**Juice and reduced juice:** Automatic juicers take the effort out of pressing the juice from fruit, but the process is easily done with a simple glass or ceramic juicer as well. Cut the fruit in half and press onto the center cone of the juicer. Or, peel the fruit, cut into 1-inch pieces, and press through a fine sieve with the back of a spoon, collecting the juice in a bowl. Squeeze citrus fruits before cutting to make extracting the juice easier. Strain juice through a fine-meshed sieve to remove any pulp, if desired.

The flavor of fruit juice can be intensified by reducing the juice: In a small saucepan over medium-high heat, bring the juice to a low boil and cook until the volume is reduced by half.

**Pulp:** Pulp is unsweetened, uncooked fruit. For pulp, pare, pit, and cut large fruit into small pieces and mash or press through a fine sieve until the pulp is a uniform texture. Berries can simply be mashed. Strain through a fine-meshed sieve to remove the seeds.

## Uncooked Fruit Purée (Coulis)
Makes about 2 cups

> 4 cups fresh berries, or 1 pound fresh fruit,
>     peeled and cut into 1/2-inch dice
> 2 tablespoons sugar or more to taste
> 1 teaspoon fresh lemon juice (optional)

Place the fruit in a food processor or blender and purée until smooth. Strain the purée through a fine-meshed sieve. Stir in sugar and lemon juice, adjusting to taste. Cover and refrigerate until needed. This purée may be used as an ingredient in another recipe, or by itself as a sauce.

## Cooked Berry Purée or Sauce
Makes about 2 cups

> 4 cups fresh berries
> 1/4 cup sugar, or more to taste
> 1/4 cup water
> 2 tablespoons raspberry liqueur or eau-de-vie
>     (optional)
> 1 tablespoon fresh lemon juice, or more to taste
> 1/2 teaspoon ground cinnamon or more to taste

Put the berries in a large sauté pan or skillet with the 1/4 cup sugar, water, and optional liqueur or eau-de-vie. Cook over medium heat for 15 minutes, or until the fruit is soft enough to mash with a spoon and most of the liquid has evaporated. Add the lemon juice and cinnamon, then taste and adjust the flavor with additional sugar, lemon juice, or cinnamon as needed.

Transfer the mixture to a blender or food processor and purée until smooth. Strain the fruit through a fine-meshed sieve, cover, and refrigerate until cold, about 2 hours; this should be a very thick purée. It may be used as an ingredient in another recipe, or by itself as a sauce.

## Blackberry Sauce
Makes 2 cups

> Zest and juice of 1/2 orange
> Zest and juice of 1/2 lemon
> 3 tablespoons raspberry liqueur
> 3 tablespoons crème de cassis
> 1 tablespoon Pernod or other anise-flavored
>     liqueur
> 1/4 cup sugar
> 1-1/2 cups fresh blackberries
> 1 vanilla bean, halved lengthwise

Combine all of the ingredients except 1/2 cup of the blackberries and the vanilla bean in a saucepan and heat over medium heat. Scrape the seeds from the vanilla bean and add the seeds and the pod to the pan. Bring to a boil and cook for 3 minutes. Strain through a fine-meshed sieve. Add the remaining whole blackberries.

# *Ice Creams and Sorbets*

## Vanilla Ice Cream
Makes 1-1/2 pints

> 2 cups heavy (whipping) cream
> 1/2 cup half-and-half
> 1 vanilla bean, halved lengthwise, or
>     1 tablespoon vanilla extract
> 8 egg yolks
> 1 cup sugar

In a heavy medium saucepan, combine the cream, half-and-half, and vanilla bean, if using. Bring to a boil over medium-high heat. Meanwhile, beat the egg yolks with the sugar in a medium bowl until light and fluffy. Slowly whisk some of the hot cream mixture into the egg yolks, then add the egg yolks to the hot cream mixture and cook over low heat, stirring constantly, until the mixture is thick enough to coat the spoon. Remove from heat and remove the vanilla bean or stir in the vanilla extract. Cover and chill for at least 2 to 3 hours.

Freeze in an ice cream maker according to the manufacturer's instructions, or see below if you do not have an ice cream freezer.

**Fruit Ice Cream:** Delete the vanilla bean or extract. Stir 1 cup fruit purée into the chilled ice cream base and freeze in an ice cream maker according to the manufacturer's instructions. Makes 1 quart.

**Macadamia Nut Ice Cream:** Freeze the ice cream in an ice cream maker according to the manufacturer's instructions until partially frozen. Blend in 1/2 cup caramel sauce (page 142) and 1 cup chopped macadamia nuts. Return to the ice cream maker until frozen. Makes 1 quart.

**Green Tea Ice Cream:** Prepare the ice cream base, placing 5 Earl Grey tea bags in the cream before it is heated. Bring the cream to a boil, remove from the heat, and let sit for 5 minutes. Remove the tea bags and proceed with the ice cream base as above.

## Fruit Sorbet

Sorbet, also called sherbet or ice, is made from fruit purée, fruit juice, and sugar syrup. The length of time the syrup cooks affects the texture of the sorbet: French sorbets are usually made with a very light syrup and are slightly grainy while Italian sorbettos are made with heavier syrup and are smoother.

> 2 pounds fresh fruit, peeled, seeded, and diced
> 1 cup simple syrup (page 159)
> Juice of 1/2 lemon

In a blender or food processor, combine the syrup and fruit and purée until smooth. Strain through a fine-meshed sieve if necessary to remove seeds. Freeze in an ice cream maker according to the manufacturer's instructions.

## Making Ice Cream Without a Machine

While there are a number of inexpensive ice cream makers on the market, it is possible to make ice creams and sorbets without any sort of machine. Here are two methods:

**Blender or food processor method:** Freeze the mixture in ice cube trays for 45 minutes to 1 hour, or until the cubes are almost frozen. Empty the ice cube trays into a blender or food processor and process, using on-and-off pulsing motions, until the mixture is smooth. Return to the ice cube trays and freeze for another 30 minutes. Process again and scrape the ice cream into a plastic container or mixing bowl. Freeze again until solid. When you are ready to serve, let stand at room temperature for several minutes to soften slightly.

**Electric mixer method:** Freeze the mixture in a mixing bowl until the outer 2 to 3 inches is frozen. Remove from the freezer and beat with an electric mixer until smooth. Repeat 2 more times, then allow to freeze completely. When you are ready to serve, let stand at room temperature for several minutes to soften slightly.

# *Mayonnaise*
Makes 1-1/2 cups

> 1 teaspoon Dijon mustard
> 2 egg yolks
> Salt and white pepper to taste
> 2 cups peanut or other vegetable oil
> 2 tablespoons white wine vinegar or fresh lemon
>     juice

Using a whisk or an electric blender, beat the mustard, egg yolks, salt, and pepper in a medium bowl until thick. Gradually whisk the oil into the egg mixture, starting with 1 drop at a time; when 2 or 3 tablespoons or the oils have been whisked into the eggs, you can pour in the rest of the oil in a fine stream while whisking constantly. Add the vinegar or lemon juice to the mixture 1 teaspoon at a time, whisking constantly until smooth. Cover and refrigerate up to 1 week.

# *Nuts*

## Shelling Macadamia Nuts

Macadamia nuts are round and extremely hard, making them very difficult to crack. They are readily available already shelled, but if you wish to do the job yourself, preheat the oven to 150°F. Spread the nuts in a single layer on a baking sheet and roast for 2 hours (very large nuts may roast for up to 4 hours). Let cool. Place a nut in the indent of a chopping block (or even a crack in the sidewalk) and rap it sharply with a small hammer. The nuts will almost always come out whole. Macadamia nuts in the shell can be husked and kept in a basket in a dry place up to 6 months. Unshelled macadamias may be frozen and used as needed. To salt them, sauté the nuts in a little butter or oil. Lightly salt them, then cool and place in an airtight jar. Or, soak the nuts in salted water overnight, then place in a single layer on a baking sheet and dry for 1 hour at 150°F.

## Toasting Nuts

Preheat the oven to 350°F. Spread the nuts in a single layer in a shallow pan. Bake, shaking the pan occasionally to toss the nuts, until golden, 5 to 12 minutes. Let cool.

## Toasting Sesame Seeds

Spread the seeds in a small dry sauté pan or skillet over high heat. Stir and toss the sesame seeds until nutty brown and fragrant, about 3 to 5 minutes.

## Glazed Nuts
Makes 2 cups

> 2 cups peeled, unsalted nuts
> 2 cups water
> 1 cup sugar

In a heavy saucepan, stir the water and sugar over low heat just until the sugar dissolves. Increase heat to medium-high and continue to cook, brushing away the crystals which form on the sides of the pan with a damp brush. Do not stir the sugar mixture. Let the mixture boil until the sugar begins to color and turns golden brown. Remove from heat immediately and gently place the pan in a bowl of ice to stop the cooking process. When the caramel has cooled slightly, dip the prepared nuts in the caramel to glaze, and set aside on aluminum foil or waxed paper. If the caramel thickens too much before use, warm it gently to melt.

## *Peppers*

Bell peppers now come in a rainbow of colors, and there are literally hundreds of varieties of chilies. Here are some general procedures common to all:

**Handling fresh chilies:** Precautions should be exercised in handling fresh chilies, since they contain potent oils. Either wear rubber gloves, or wash your hands thoroughly with soap and hot water after handling chilies. Never touch your skin until you've washed your hands. Also, wash the knife and cutting board in hot soapy water. Do not handle hot chilies under running water, since that spreads the oil vapors upward to your eyes.

**Seeding and deribbing:** Either cut out the ribs and seeds with a paring knife, or cut away the flesh, leaving a skeleton of ribs and seeds to discard. For the second method, cut a slice off the bottom of the pepper or chili so that it will stand up on the cutting board. Holding the pepper or chili with your free hand, slice its natural curvature in sections. You will be left with all the flesh and none of the seeds and ribs. The flesh may now be cut as indicated in the recipe.

**Roasting and peeling:** Cut a small slit near the stem end of each whole pepper or chili to ensure that it will not explode. Roast the peppers or chilies in one of the following ways:

• For a large number of peppers or chilies, and to retain the most texture, lower them gently into 375°F (almost smoking) oil and fry until the skin blisters. Turn them with tongs when one side is blistered, since they will float to the surface of the oil. This method is also the most effective if the vegetables are not perfectly shaped, since it is difficult to get the heat from the broiler into the folds of peppers and some chilies.

• Preheat the broiler. Cut the peppers or chilies into quarters lengthwise and place them on a broiler or rack 6 inches from the heat source, turning them with tongs until all surfaces are charred.
• Put the peppers or chilies on the cooking rack of a hot charcoal or gas grill and turn them until the skin is charred.

• Place a wire cake rack over a gas or electric burner set at the highest temperature and turn the peppers or chilies with tongs until all surfaces are charred.

Cool the peppers or chilies by one of the following methods:

• Put them in ice water. This stops the cooking action immediately and cools them enough to peel them within 1 minute. The peppers or chilies will stay relatively firm.

• Put the peppers or chilies in a paper bag, close it, and let them cool. This also effectively separates the flesh from the skin, but it will be about 20 minutes before they are cool enough to handle, and they will soften somewhat during that time. Finally, pull the skin off and remove the seeds.

## Chili Pepper Water
Makes 3 cups

Bottles of homemade chili pepper water are a staple on Hawaiian tables. At its most basic, chili pepper water consists of fresh chilies, rice vinegar, and garlic, bottled and aged for 2 to 3 weeks. This version shows its Asian influence with ginger. Chili pepper water can be purchased at markets in Hawai'i and through mail order services.

> 2-1/2 cups boiling water
> 3/4 cup cold water
> 2 tablespoons distilled white vinegar
> 1 garlic clove, minced
> 1 tablespoon chopped fresh ginger
> 14 Hawaiian or Thai chilies

In a blender or food processor, combine all ingredients and purée until smooth, about 1 minute. Pour into hot sterilized bottles, cover, and refrigerate.

# Rice

**Steamed rice:** Place the rice in a large saucepan. Cover with water and rinse twice. Drain. Add water to cover the rice by one inch. Cover the saucepan and bring to a boil over medium-high heat. Boil 1 minute. Reduce the heat to low and steam 10 minutes. Reduce heat to very low and steam for 10 minutes more. Or, line the basket of a bamboo steamer with 2 layers of cheesecloth. Place the rinsed rice in the lined basket, cover the basket, and place over boiling water, making sure the steaming basket does not touch the water. Steam for 20 minutes, or until the rice is tender to the bite. One cup of dry rice will serve 4 people when cooked.

**Steamed Jasmine Rice:** Jasmine rice is a long-grained variety with a slight jasmine scent. Steam as above.

**Steamed Sticky Rice:** Use glutinous rice, a short-grained variety frequently used in Asian dishes. Place the rice in a large bowl and cover with cold water. Rub the rice between your hands and drain off the water. Cover the rice with clean water and repeat until the water runs clear. Cover the rice with water and soak overnight, or, soak the rice in hot water for 3 hours before steaming. Drain the rice. Place in a cheesecloth-lined steaming basket or a steamer. Place over boiling water, making sure the steaming basket does not touch the water. Cover and steam 30 minutes. Three cups of glutinous rice will serve 4 people when cooked.

# Roasting Garlic

With a sharp knife, cut the top quarter off a head of unpeeled garlic. Rub the head with olive oil. Place in a baking dish in a 350°F oven and roast for 1 hour. Let cool to the touch. Separate the cloves from the head and squeeze the roasted garlic pulp or purée from each.

# Rendering Duck Fat

Pull the yellow fat away from the skin and meat of the duck and put it in a heavy, medium sauté pan or skillet. Cook slowly over low heat, letting the fat melt. When all the fat has drained away from the tissue and the tissue is brown and crisp, strain the fat through a fine-meshed sieve or cheesecloth into a small heat-proof bowl. Use immediately, or, let the fat cool, cover, and refrigerate.

# Scallion-Infused Oil

In a medium bowl, combine 2 minced whole scallions with 1 cup extra-virgin olive oil. Cover and let sit for at least 48 hours. Strain through a fine-meshed sieve into a glass jar or bottle; cover.

# Seafood

Select the freshest fish available. Look for fish with bulging, not sunken, eyes, and a sweet fresh smell (shark, squid, and skates, exceptions to the rule, will have a slightly ammoniated smell when fresh). Store fresh fish in the coldest part of the refrigerator, wrapping in plastic wrap and placing on ice chips if necessary. Lean fish keeps longer than fatty fish, but in no case keep it longer than 2 days. Freeze fish immediately to keep it longer. Do not freeze fish that has already been frozen.

**Cleaning Squid:** Press the body from the top end toward the tentacles to squeeze out the entrails and quill. Discard the quill. Rinse under cold water, cut off the tentacles just above the eyes, and squeeze the tentacles to eject the horny beak. Discard the beak. Pull the skin from the body with your fingers. Pull the wings from the sides and skin them also. Chop the tentacles into rings if desired.

**Peeling and Deveining Shrimp:** Rinse under cold water and break the head portion from the body and tail. Pull off the legs on the underside. With your fingers or a small knife, split the shell on the underside and peel it back over the shrimp. You can pull off the small tail at this time, or break the shell away from the tail and leave the small tail attached. With a small, sharp knife, split the top of the back of the shrimp and lift out the black strip.

# Smoking

Arrange your smoker or charcoal grill for smoking: You want indirect heat and a low fire with barely enough oxygen to burn. In a charcoal grill, place the charcoal to one side of the grill, ignite it and let it burn until white ash forms on the briquettes. Add selected wood for smoke flavor, (hickory, mesquite, apple, etc.). Only a few small pieces are needed, about the equivalent of 4 charcoal briquets. Wood shavings or a small amount of sawdust work well. Place a rack over the fire area. In a gas grill, light the gas, turn to low flame, and place the wood chips over the fire area. Place the food to be smoked on the opposite side of the grill from the fire. Cover, open the air vents in the bottom of the grill, and nearly close the vents in the top of the grill.

# Stocks

## Chicken Stock
Makes 12 cups

      6 quarts water
      5 pounds bony chicken parts, skin, and
         trimmings
      2 carrots, peeled and cut into chunks

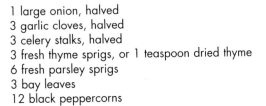

1 large onion, halved
3 garlic cloves, halved
3 celery stalks, halved
3 fresh thyme sprigs, or 1 teaspoon dried thyme
6 fresh parsley sprigs
3 bay leaves
12 black peppercorns

In a large stockpot, combine the water and the chicken parts, skin, and trimmings. Bring to a boil, then reduce heat to a simmer, skimming off the foam that rises for the first 10 to 15 minutes. Cook for 1 hour, then add the remaining ingredients. Bring to a boil, reduce heat to low, and simmer the stock for 3 hours.

Strain the stock through a fine-meshed sieve and let cool to room temperature, then refrigerate. Remove and discard the congealed layer of fat on the surface. Store in the refrigerator up to 3 days. To keep longer, bring the stock to a boil every 3 days, or freeze it for up to 3 months.

**To clarify the stock:** Let the stock cool until it is lukewarm. Blend 3 egg whites together and pour into the warm stock; as the whites coagulate and rise they will trap bits still floating in the stock. When the egg whites have risen to the top and the stock is clear, skim the eggs off the top with a slotted spoon. You can repeat the process if necessary to obtain clear stock.

## Veal or Beef Stock
Makes 12 cups

8 pounds veal or beef bones and trimmings
2 onions, halved
2 carrots, peeled and cut into chunks
2 celery stalks, halved
3 garlic cloves, halved
8 quarts water
3 fresh thyme sprigs, or 1 teaspoon dried thyme
6 fresh parsley sprigs
2 bay leaves
12 black peppercorns

Preheat the oven to 400°F. Put the bones and trimmings in a roasting pan and roast about 45 minutes, turning occasionally. Add the vegetables to the pan and roast for 20 minutes, or until the vegetables are browned.

Place the bones and vegetables in a large stockpot, pouring off any fat. Add 1 quart of the water to the pan and place on the stove over high heat. Stir to scrape up the brown bits clinging to the bottom of the pan. Pour this liquid into the stockpot with the remaining 7 quarts water and the herbs and spices. Bring to a boil, then reduce heat to a

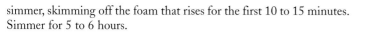

simmer, skimming off the foam that rises for the first 10 to 15 minutes. Simmer for 5 to 6 hours.

Strain the stock through a fine-meshed sieve and discard the solids. Let cool, then refrigerate. Remove and discard the congealed layer of fat on the surface. Store in the refrigerator up to 3 days. To keep longer, bring the stock to a boil every 3 days, or freeze it for up to 3 months.

## Fish Stock
Makes 12 cups

> 4 quarts water
> 1 cup dry white wine
> 4 pounds fish trimmings such as skin, bones, and
>     heads
> 2 tablespoons fresh lemon juice
> 1 onion, halved
> 2 celery stalks, halved
> 4 fresh parsley sprigs
> 2 fresh thyme sprigs, or 1 teaspoon dried thyme
> 2 bay leaves
> 6 black peppercorns

In a large stockpot, bring the water and wine to a boil. Rinse all the fish trimmings under cold running water, add to the stockpot, and return to a boil. Reduce heat to a simmer, skimming off the foam that rises for the first 10 to 15 minutes. Simmer for 1 hour.

Add the remaining ingredients to the pot. Bring the mixture to a boil, then reduce heat to a simmer and cook for 1-1/2 to 2 hours. Strain the stock through a fine-meshed sieve, pressing on the solids with the back of a large spoon. Discard the solids. Let cool, then cover and refrigerate up to 3 days. To keep longer, bring the stock to a boil every 3 days, or freeze it for up to 3 months.

## Duck Stock
Makes 12 cups

> 3 pounds duck trimmings (bones, skin, fat,
>     and/or anything else you can trim away)
>     and meat
> 4 quarts water
> 1 onion, halved
> 1 carrot, peeled and halved
> 2 celery stalks, including leaves, cut into sections
> 3 fresh thyme sprigs, or 1 teaspoon dried thyme
> 3 fresh parsley sprigs
> 6 black peppercorns

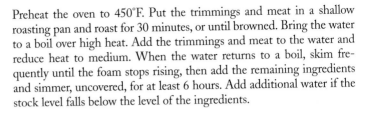

Preheat the oven to 450°F. Put the trimmings and meat in a shallow roasting pan and roast for 30 minutes, or until browned. Bring the water to a boil over high heat. Add the trimmings and meat to the water and reduce heat to medium. When the water returns to a boil, skim frequently until the foam stops rising, then add the remaining ingredients and simmer, uncovered, for at least 6 hours. Add additional water if the stock level falls below the level of the ingredients.

Strain the stock and discard the solids. Let the stock cool to room temperature, then refrigerate. Remove and discard the congealed fat layer from the top. Store in the refrigerator for up to 3 days. To keep longer, bring to a boil every 3 days, or refrigerate for up to 3 months.

## Veal or Beef Demi-Glacé
Makes 2 cups

Demi-glacé is unsalted meat stock that has been degreased and then reduced over medium-low heat until it becomes rich and syrupy. The concentrated flavor adds richness and depth to sauces and stews. Traditional demi-glacé is thickened with flour and must simmer gently with much tending, but this quick version is lighter and can be made more quickly because it is thickened at the end with arrowroot or cornstarch.

> 2 tablespoons vegetable oil
> 1 large onion, diced
> 2 celery stalks, diced
> 1 carrot, peeled and sliced
> 1/2 cup diced ham
> 3 tablespoons tomato paste
> 1 fresh thyme sprig
> 1 bay leaf
> 6 peppercorns
> 10 cups veal or beef stock (page 156)
> 1/2 cup Madeira
> 2 to 3 teaspoons arrowroot or cornstarch mixed
>     with 2 tablespoons cold water
> Salt and freshly ground black pepper to taste
> 1 tablespoon unsalted butter

Heat the oil in a large saucepan over medium heat. Stir in the onion, celery, carrot, and ham. Cover and cook over low heat for 10 minutes. Uncover the pan and stir in the tomato paste, thyme, bay leaf, and peppercorns. Whisk in the stock and Madeira, and bring to a boil over high heat.

Once the mixture has started to boil, reduce heat to medium high and cook the sauce to reduce to 2 cups. Depending on the rate at which the liquid is boiling, this may take anywhere from 30 minutes to 1 hour. Strain the liquid through a fine-meshed sieve into a 2-cup measuring cup. If it has not reduced enough, pour the liquid back into the pan and keep boiling. If it has reduced too much, add enough water to make 2 cups.

Pour the liquid back into the pan and bring it back to a simmer. Whisk in the arrowroot or cornstarch mixture 1 teaspoon at a time, returning the sauce to a simmer after each addition, until the sauce reaches the desired consistency. Add salt and pepper. If using the sauce immediately, swirl in the butter. If not serving immediately, do not whisk in the butter, but remove the pan from heat and place dots of butter on the surface of the sauce to prevent a skin from forming. Whisk in the butter when reheating the sauce. To store, cover and refrigerate for up to 5 days or freeze for up to 3 months.

# *Sugar*

## Simple Syrup
Makes 3 cups

> 2 cups sugar
> 1 cup water

In a heavy, medium saucepan, combine the sugar and water and cook over high heat until the sugar dissolves and the mixture reaches a full boil, about 3 minutes. Remove from heat, let cool, and store in a covered container in the refrigerator for up to 3 weeks.

## Pulled Sugar

Pulled sugar is definitely in the "advanced" category of confectionery. Yet it makes spectacular garnishes, and, once pulled and worked into a shiny mass, it can be kept for months if you place it on a piece of clean limestone in an airtight container. Keep it workable by placing it under a heat lamp until warm, soft, and pliable.

> 4 pounds sugar
> 2 cups water
> 1 teaspoon cream of tartar
> Food coloring, if desired

In a heavy, medium saucepan, combine the sugar, water, and cream of tartar and bring to a boil over medium heat. Cook until the syrup reaches 160°F. Do not stir the syrup during this time. When the temperature has reached 160°F, remove the pan from heat and set it in a pan of ice water to stop the cooking. The syrup will still be colorless.

When the syrup has cooled slightly, pour it out onto a marble slab or a baking sheet. Let it continue to cool. If desired, drop 4 or 5 large drops of food coloring randomly over the surface of the syrup as it cools. Brown coloring will result in a golden color; all colors will lighten

considerably as the sugar is worked. When it appears to have thickened, put on heavy rubber gloves and lift the edges of the syrup; the syrup will pull away from slab and fold back on itself. Use the palm of your hand to roll the edges in over the remainder of the syrup. Continue to lift the syrup over itself again and again, working slowly at first, then faster as the sugar cools. As it becomes cool enough to pull, it will hold its shape. When it is cool enough to handle, grasp the lump with both hands, lift it, and quickly pull your hands apart, stretching the sugar. Let the center of the strip rest on the work surface and fold the ends across, folding the sugar strip in thirds. Lift again with both hands and twist as if you are wringing it. Repeat the pulling, folding, and twisting motions about 45 times, or until the sugar develops a deep shine (overpulling the sugar will kill the shine). It will look like mother of pearl. The wringing action helps distribute the color evenly throughout the mass; if you prefer the effect of fine straight lines of color, do not wring between foldings. Place the sugar mass under a heat lamp to keep it pliable.

- **To make leaves or petals:** Using scissors, cut off a small piece of the sugar and press it into a leaf mold or other form. If creating flowers, press several of these "petals" together to form the flower.

- **To make spirals:** Working under the heat lamp, pull a piece of sugar from the lump and press it against a wooden dowel or spoon handle. Holding the sugar in place with your thumb, twist the dowel, pulling it away from the sugar to draw a thin twisting strand from the mass, until the desired length is reached. Pinch off the end from the lump, remove from the lamp area to let cool, and slide the finished spiral off the dowel.

- **To make ribbons:** Working under the heat lamp, grasp a piece of sugar and pull a long, thin strip from the lump. Pinch or cut it off, stretch it as thin as desired, and twist and ruffle as desired. Remove from the lamp area and let cool.

## Tomatoes

### Smoked Tomatoes

Arrange your smoker or charcoal grill for smoking (see page 155). Cut plum (Roma) tomatoes in half lengthwise, sprinkle with salt, and place on the rack cut-side up on the side away from the fire. Cover, open the air vents in the bottom of the grill, and nearly close the vents in the top of the grill. Smoke until the tomatoes are almost dry and have absorbed the smoky flavor, 45 to 60 minutes.

**To peel and seed tomatoes:** Cut out the core of the tomato. With a knife, make an X on the bottom of the tomato. Plunge the tomato into boiling water for exactly 10 seconds. Remove with a slotted spoon and plunge into a bowl of cold water, then drain. Peel off the skin. Cut the tomato in half crosswise. Squeeze and shake the tomato gently over a bowl or sink to remove the seeds. Any clinging seeds may be removed with the tip of a paring knife or your finger.

## Preparing Ti Leaves

With a sharp knife, remove the stiff back of the leaf rib, starting at the tip. Do not cut the leaf itself. With the rib removed, the leaf will be pliable enough to wrap food in packages tied with the removed rib or kitchen string.

## Vegetable Curls

To curl carrots, beets, and radishes for garnish, grate or pare the cleaned vegetable in long thin strips and immediately place the strips in ice water. To curl green onions (scallions), with a small sharp knife, cut in half lengthwise through the bulb. Trim the stems 4 to 5 inches above the bulb. Cut the green stems into lengthwise strips, leaving attached at the bulb, and place in ice water.

# Glossary of Ingredients

### ■ ■ ■

The ingredients used in Hawaiian recipes come from all over the world. It is a challenge to find the perfect ingredient, but nearly all, no matter how exotic, can be located—or a suitable alternative can be located. This extensive glossary will help you understand the international lexicon of Hawaiian ingredients. The mail order section which follows will help you obtain the most unusual items.

## A

**'Ahi:**
The Hawaiian name for both yellowfin and bigeye tuna. Often served in the islands as sashimi (Japanese-style raw fish).

**Aku:**
The Hawaiian name for skipjack tuna. Deep red in color and stronger tasting than 'ahi. Good broiled, or grilled, or used raw in poke.

**Amaranth:**
A slightly sweet vegetable with small dark green leaves and a red stem. An ancient Chinese food and a symbol of immortality. Also called Chinese spinach, the leaves have a watercress-like flavor and are used throughout Asia.

**Anaheim chili:**
Long green narrow chili used often in Southwest cuisines.

**Ancho chili:**
The dried poblano chili, dark red and usually 4 to 6 inches long.

**Asian sesame oil:**
A strong-flavored oil made from toasted sesame seeds and used in most Asian cuisines. Only a small amount is needed for flavoring. Sesame oil burns at a lower heat than most oils. Refrigerate after opening.

**Au:**
The Hawaiian name for swordfish, or marlin.

**Azuki beans:**
Reddish beans used in Chinese and Japanese cuisine, often in sweet pastries. Look for them in an Asian grocery.

## B

**Baby corn:**
Miniature ears of corn 2 or 3 inches long. Also called young corn. If fresh baby corn is not available it can be found canned in most Asian markets.

**Bamboo shoots:**
Young, cone-shaped shoots sold fresh or in cans in Asian groceries.

**Bean sprouts:**
Mung beans that have sprouted. Available fresh or canned.

**Bean thread noodles:**
Also called cellophane noodles, glass noodles, or Chinese long rice, these noodles are reconstituted in water before using.

**Black sesame seeds:**
Also called goma. Available in bottles or packages in Asian markets.

**Bok choy:**
A Chinese cabbage with a white stem and dark green leaves. You can substitute napa cabbage if not available.

**Breadfruit:**
A bland, starchy vegetable widely used in the Pacific, but difficult to get on the U.S. mainland. Potatoes are a good substitute.

# C

**Cajun spice mix:**
A hot dry spice of black pepper, paprika, cayenne, and other spices. Available bottled in most markets.

**Char siu:**
Pork or beef that has been marinated in a sweet-spicy red sauce and dried. Used in small amounts to flavor noodle dishes or as a side dish.

**Chili oil:**
An Asian oil seasoned with hot chili peppers. Substitute any hot sauce.

**Chili paste:**
A thick chili sauce produced and used in many Asian cuisines such as Thai, Vietnamese, Indonesian, and Filipino. It is made of chilis, onions, sugar, and tamarind.

**Chili pepper water:**
A hot mixture of small red chilies, salt, vinegar, and garlic. It may be purchased in bottle form, or see the recipe on page 153.

**Chinese broccoli:**
See choi sum.

**Chinese cabbage:**
See won bok.

**Chinese fermented black beans:**
Salted fermented black beans. They can be purchased bottled or in cans in Asian markets, and should be rinsed and chopped to release their flavor.

**Chinese five spice powder:**
A spice mix of anise, cinnamon, cloves, fennel, and star anise. Available in Asian markets.

**Chinese long rice:**
See bean thread noodles.

**Chinese mustard cabbage:**
Also known as gai choy; mustard greens may be substituted.

**Chinese parsley:**
See cilantro.

**Chinese peas:**
Also known as snow peas.

**Choi sum:**
Chinese broccoli. If not available, substitute napa cabbage or regular broccoli.

**Cilantro:**
A pungent flat-leaf herb resembling parsley; also called fresh coriander or Chinese parsley.

**Coconut milk:**
A liquid extracted from shredded coconut meat by soaking it with hot water and straining. Available in cans from Southeast Asia, or see the recipe on page 145.

**Curry (kari) leaves:**
Small, shiny fragrant leaves resembling bay leaves used prominently in Sri Lankan cooking. Used fresh or dried. The fresh leaves are pulverized and fried in oil to release a currylike flavor. Available in Asian markets. Substitute a pinch of curry powder.

# D

**Daikon:**
Japanese name for a white, crisp radish. Turnips can be substituted.

**Dashi:**
Commercially available powdered Japanese soup stock. Available in Asian markets.

**Date palm sugar:**
A rich, brown, sugar made of ground dried dates, often made into flat bars, or

added to soy sauce to make a sweet sauce. Available in Asian markets.

# E

**Edible flowers:**
Flowers add a beautiful touch to dishes, and many flowers are edible. Make sure they are free of pesticides: your own garden is your surest supplier. Among edible blooms are pansies, violas, and violets; roses, apple, peach, and plum blooms; geraniums; orange and lemon blossoms; nasturtiums; lavender, jasmine, daises, daylilies, dianthus, marigolds, and squash blooms.

# F

**Fiddlehead ferns:**
Known as pohole, or warabi, or hōʻiʻo fern in Hawaii. Available in specialty markets. Substitute haricots verts or baby Blue Lake green beans.

**Fish sauce:**
Also called nam pla in Thai cuisine or nuoc mam in Vietnamese cuisine. Very salty and pungent. Made from fermented small fish and shrimp. Available in Asian markets.

**Furikake:**
A spicy Japanese seaweed-based seasoning mix.

# G

**Galangal:**
Also called Thai ginger or galangha. A large, juicy rhizome with a thin pinkish-brown skin. Substitute fresh ginger.

**Ginger:**
Fresh ginger is a brown, fibrous, knobby rhizome. It keeps for long periods of time. To use, peel the brown outside skin and slice, chop, or purée. It will keep indefinitely placed in a jar with sherry and refrigerated.

**Goma:**
See black sesame seeds.

**Green curry paste:**
A blend of chilies and other seasonings, including lime and coriander, used in Thai cuisine and available packaged or in jars. Substitute curry powder.

**Green papaya:**
The unripe form of the papaya, usually shredded and used in salads and stir-fries in Southeast Asian cuisines.

**Guava:**
A round tropical fruit with a yellow skin and pink inner flesh and many seeds. Grown commercially in Hawaiʻi. The purée or juice is available as a frozen concentrate. Guava can also be made into jams, jellies, and sauces.

**Gyoza:**
A Japanese dumpling, also known as a pot sticker.

# H

**Hāhā:**
The Hawaiian word for the stem of the taro plant. See taro.

**Hajikami:**
Pickled ginger sprouts, used in Japanese cooking as a garnish. Available bottled in Japanese markets.

**Haupia:**
Traditional Hawaiian pudding made of coconut milk, sugar, and cornstarch.

**Hawaiian chili:**
Small, hot, red chili pepper. Substitute Thai chilies or red pepper flakes.

**Hawaiian salt:**
A coarse sea salt gathered in tidal pools after a storm or high tide. Hawaiians sometimes mix it with a red clay to make alae salt. Substitute kosher salt.

**Hearts of palm:**
Tender palm shoots, sometimes available fresh, but most often found in cans in Asian markets. Used mostly in salads and stir-fries.

**Hō'i'o fern:**
See fiddlehead ferns.

**Hoisin sauce:**
A thick, brownish, sweet sauce made from soybean paste, sugar, and spices. Can be purchased bottled.

# I

**Ichimi:**
See togarashi.

**Imu:**
A firepit, or underground oven, of hot volcanic stones, used in Hawaiian cooking to steam food.

**Inamona sauce:**
A traditional Hawaiian seasoning paste of kukui nuts, salt, and chilies.

# J

**Japanese eggplant:**
A long, narrow, purple, eggplant. Substitute Italian eggplant.

**Japanese plum wine:**
Wine made from the Japanese plum, or ume, and available in Asian and specialty foods stores.

**Jasmine rice:**
A fragrant and delicate Asian rice. Substitute white long-grained rice.

**Jícama:**
A bulbous, turnip-like root used raw in salads or cooked as a vegetable. Available in Asian and Latino markets.

# K

**Kaffir lime leaves:**
Citrus-flavored leaves sold in Asian markets. Used widely in Southeast Asian dishes. Sold fresh or dried. Reconstitute dried leaves by soaking in warm water. Substitute grated lime zest.

**Kahuku prawns:**
Farm-raised, freshwater prawns that are slightly sweeter than shrimp. Jumbo shrimp may be substituted.

**Kaiware sprouts:**
A sharp-flavored sprout used in Japanese dishes.

**Kajiki:**
The Japanese name for Pacific blue marlin. Substitute swordfish or shark.

**Kalo:**
The Hawaiian word for taro root. See taro.

**Kālua pig:**
Shredded pork that has been cooked in a traditional underground pit, or imu.

**Ka'u orange:**
A variety of orange grown on the island of Hawai'i. The outer skin is ugly and blackened, but the inside is especially sweet and juicy. Substitute Valencia oranges.

**Keāhole baby lobster:**
Small, freshwater-farmed lobsters grown in the Kona district of the island of Hawai'i. Substitute spiny lobsters or jumbo prawns.

**Kecap manis:**
A thick, dark, Indonesian soy sauce sweetened with palm sugar. Available in Asian markets.

**Kiawe tree:**
The Hawaiian name for the mesquite tree, a source of excellent charcoal.

**Kiwi:**
Kiwis hide their sweet green flesh in a fuzzy brown skin. Select fruit with few imperfections in the skin, and no very soft bruised spots. Peel the kiwi and slice; the seeds are edible.

**Kukui nuts:**
A native Hawaiian nut very high in oil. Used roasted, salted, or pounded in traditional Hawaiian cooking.

**Kulolo:**
A traditional Hawaiian pudding made with taro and brown sugar.

**Kūmū:**
A reef fish and a member of the goat-fish family. Its meat is mild and delicate. Substitute any white meat fish with a high fat content, such as flounder or halibut.

## L

**Lauae fern:**
A shiny, smooth fern used as a border in Hawaiian gardens, and as decorations for parties.

**Laulau:**
A bundle of meat, fish, and taro leaves wrapped in ti leaves and steamed. A traditional Hawaiian dish.

**Lemon-scented basil:**
A leafy aromatic herb used in Southeast Asian cooking.

**Lemongrass:**
Long greenish stalks with a pungent lemony flavor. Also called citronella. Substitute grated lemon zest.

**Liliko'i:**
The Hawaiian name for passion fruit, which is a small yellow, purple, or brown oval fruit of the passion fruit vine. The "passion" in passion fruit comes from the fact that its flower resembles a Maltese cross and refers to Christ's crucifixion, not to aphrodesiac qualities. The flavor is delicate but somewhat sharp, and perfumelike. Passion fruit is a natural substitute for lemon juice. Passion fruit concentrate can be found in the frozen juice section of many markets. Substitute oranges.

**Limu:**
The Hawaiian word for seaweed, of which they use as many as twenty-five varieties. Japanese ogo is a type of sea-weed. Much ogo today is farm raised.

**Lingham chili sauce:**
A hot sweet sauce from Malaysia, made from chilies, onions, sugar, and spices. Substitute any sweet hot chili sauce or paste.

**Lomi lomi salmon:**
A fresh-tasting Hawaiian salad of salt-cured salmon, onion, and tomato.

**Lotus root:**
The root of the Chinese water lily. Available fresh or canned in Chinese markets.

**Lū'au:**
A traditional Hawaiian feast that usually includes foods prepared in an imu, or underground oven. See page 165.

**Lū'au leaves:**
The young, green tops of the taro root. Substitute fresh spinach.

**Lumpia wrappers:**
Thin rectangular noodle sheets used to make lumpia, the Filipino version of pot stickers. Substitute eggroll skins.

**Lundberg rice mix:**
A packaged mix of wild and premium brown rices produced by the Lundberg family of California. Available in special-ty foods stores. Substitute any wild and brown rice mix.

**Lychee:**
A small fruit with white meat and a hard shell Available fresh and canned in Asian markets.

## M

**Macadamia nuts:**
A rich, oily nut grown mostly on the Big Island of Hawai'i. Native to Australia. They're good, but expensive, canned.

**Macadamia nut oil:**
A premium cooking and salad oil pro-duced in Hawai'i from macadamia nuts. It has a high heat threshold for burning.

**Mahimahi:**
Also called dolphinfish, with a firm pink flesh. Best fresh, but often available frozen. A standard in island restaurants and markets. Substitute snapper, catfish, or halibut.

**Mango:**
Gold and green tropical fruit available in many supermarkets. Available fresh June through September in Hawai'i. Substitute fresh peaches.

**Maui onion:**
A very sweet, juicy, large, round onion similiar to the Vidalia or Walla Walla onion. Often available on the West Coast, but expensive. Substitute any sweet white onion.

**Mirin:**
A sweet Japanese rice wine found in Asian markets. Substitute sweet sherry.

**Miso:**
A soybean paste made by salting and fermenting soybeans and rice. Shiro miso, or white miso, is the mildest of several different types. Available shrink-wrapped, and in cans and jars, in Asian markets. Can be stored for months in a refrigerator.

**Mizuna:**
Japanese cabbage. Available in Asian markets and natural foods stores. Substitute fresh spinach.

**Moana:**
Also called moano; a member of the goatfish family with delicate, white meat. Substitute any white meat fish with lots of fat content.

**Mochiko sweet rice flour:**
Japanese glutinous rice flour used in making pastries and some sauces.

**Moloka'i sweet potatoes:**
Grown in small quantities on the island of Moloka'i. Substitute any sweet potato.

**Momiji chili sauce:**
A sauce of grated daikon and red pepper. Available in Asian markets.

## N

**Nam pla:**
See fish sauce.

**Napa cabbage:**
See won bok.

**Noodles**
**Bean thread noodles:**
Also called glass noodles, cellophane noodles, and long rice, these extremely fine, transparent noodles are made from mung bean starch and sold in skeins. They are soaked in water for a few seconds before cooking, and are used in salad, stir-fry, and soup.

**Chinese egg noodles:**
Made of wheat flour and egg, these noodles come in several widths and can be bought fresh or dried. They are eaten warm or cold, or cooked, made into noodle cakes, and fried.

**Rice stick noodles:**
Thin rice noodles usually sold coiled in the package. When dropped into hot oil they puff up into cruchy sticks.

**Soba Japanese buckwheat flour noodles:**
Soba noodles are light brown and thin. They are eaten warm or cold.

**Somen:**
Japanese wheat flour noodles, white in color, and very thin. Somen noodles are usually eaten cold.

**Nori:**
Sheets of dried and compressed seaweed used in making rolled sushi. Available in Asian markets.

## O

**Ogo:**
The Japanese name for seaweed.

**Okinawan sweet potato:**
A sweet potato with purple flesh. Substitute any yam or sweet potato.

**Onaga:**
The Japanese name for red snapper. Best steamed, baked, or sautéed. Substitute monkfish or orange roughy.

**Ono:**
A mackerel with white firm flesh. Also

known as wahoo. Substitute tuna, swordfish, or shark.

**Opah:**
A very large moonfish. Substitute swordfish.

**ʻŌpakapaka:**
A pink snapper with a delicate flavor. Good poached, baked, or sautéed. Substitute any red snapper, sea bass, or monkfish.

**Opal basil:**
A purple-tinged basil used in Asian cooking.

**ʻOpihi:**
A small limpet gathered from the rocks along the Hawaiian coast. Most often eaten raw, but sometimes grilled. Similar to a snail in texture and an oyster in flavor. Because of the difficulty in gathering ʻopihi, they are considered a rare delicacy.

**Oyster Sauce:**
A concentrated sauce made from oyster juice and salt, used in many Chinese and other Asian dishes. Keeps a long time in the refrigerator.

# P

**Panko:**
A crispy large-flaked Japanese bread crumb that adds more texture than ordinary bread crumbs. Found in Asian markets.

**Papaya:**
The most common papaya used in Hawaiʻi is the solo papaya, a tropical fruit with a yellow flesh, black seeds, and a perfumey scent. Other types are larger, and may have pink flesh; all are suitable for island recipes. Also see green papaya.

**Passion fruit:**
See lilikoʻi. Passion fruit juice concentrate can be found in the frozen juice section of some markets. Substitute orange juice concentrate.

**Patis fish sauce:**
A strong-flavored seasoning sauce used in Southeast Asian cuisines. Tiparos® is one brand name.

**Persimmon:**
Tart, red-orange fruit of the persimmon tree. Fuyu and Hachiqa are the most common varieties found in markets. Fuyu persimmons are small, resembling tomatoes, and may be eaten when still firm. Hachiqa are larger, the size of peaches, and must be fully ripe before being used. Persimmons are fall fruit, but may also be found dried in natural foods stores and Asian markets.

**Pickled ginger:**
Thinly sliced ginger preserved in rice wine vinegar.

**Pineapple:**
Fresh pineapples are covered with a prickly, brown skin, and topped with sharp, pointed leaves. To select a fresh ripe pineapple, give the tiny center leaves at the top a light tug. The leaves will easily pluck out of a ripe pineapple. Fresh pineapple contains an enzyme which will break down protein; rinse well and add as close to serving time as possible when using in dishes containing gelatin.

**Pipikaula:**
The Hawaiian version of beef jerky.

**Plum sauce:**
Also called Chinese plum sauce. A sweet and sour sauce available in most Asian markets.

**Plum wine:**
See Japanese plum wine.

**Poha:**
The Hawaiian name for cape gooseberries, marble-sized tart berries encased in a papery husk.

**Pohole fern:**
See fiddlehead ferns.

**Poi:**
A starchy paste made by pounding the

taro root with water until it reaches a smooth consistency. A staple in the traditional Hawaiian diet.

**Poke:**
A traditional Hawaiian dish made of raw fish, Hawaiian salt, seaweed, and chilies.

**Portuguese sausage:**
Linguiça, a pork sausage spiced with chili. Substitute hot Italian sausages.

**Pot sticker wrappers:**
Thin, round, pastry skins made from flour and water. Used to make Chinese dim sum.

**Puna goat cheese:**
A fresh white goat cheese produced in the Puna district of the island of Hawai'i. It is made in the traditional French way. Substitute any fresh white goat cheese.

**Purple potatoes:**
See Okinawan sweet potatoes.

# R

**Rice noodles:**
Also called rice vermicelli. When they are deep-fried they expand immediately to several times their size. They can also be soaked and served as soft noodles. Packages of the dry noodles are in Asian markets.

**Rice paper:**
Thin sheets of noodles made from rice flour and water. Soften the sheets in water before wrapping food with them.

**Rice wine vinegar:**
A light vinegar made from fermented rice.

# S

**Sake:**
Clear Japanese rice wine. Other strong clear liquors, such as tequila or vodka, can be substituted.

**Sambal olek:**
A chunky red chili paste used in Indonesia and Malaysia. Any Asian hot chili paste can be substituted.

**Sansho peppercorns:**
An expensive bottled peppercorn found in Japanese markets. Substitute any fine quality peppercorn, or Sichuan peppercorns.

**Sapote:**
The sapote is large, the size of an avocado, with a rough brown skin. Look for unblemished skin and a slight softness under the skin when pressed gently.

**Sesame seeds:**
Small, flat, oval, white or black seeds used to flavor or garnish main dishes and desserts.

**Shichimi:**
A Japanese spice blend of chilies, sesame seeds, orange peel, seaweed, and poppy seeds. Substitute Cajun spice mix.

**Shiitake mushrooms:**
The second most widely cultivated mushroom in the world, medium to large with umbrella-shaped, flopped tan to dark brown caps with edges that tend to roll under. Shiitakes have a woodsy, smoky flavor. Can be purchased fresh or dried in Asian groceries. To reconstitute the dried variety, soak in warm water for 30 minutes before using. Stem both fresh and dried shiitakes.

**Shiso leaf:**
Also called the beefsteak leaf, the 2- to 3-inch aromatic red-and-green leaf is very popular in Japanese cuisine. Substitute fresh basil or mint.

**Shoyu:**
The Japanese and Hawaiian name for soy sauce.

**Shutome:**
The Hawaiian broadbill swordfish. Substitute any swordfish.

**Soba noodles:**
Thin brown noodles made from buck-

wheat and wheat flour. They cook quickly and can be served hot or cold.

**Solo papaya:**
A small yellow papaya with orange flesh and black seeds. The most common variety found in Hawai'i.

**Soy sauce:**
A dark salty liquid made from soybeans, flour, salt, and water. Dark soy sauce is stronger than light soy sauce. A staple in most Asian cuisines.

**Spicy tobiko:**
Japanese caviar seasoned with wasabi.

**Sprouts:**
Bean, daikon, pea, sunflower, and radish are all types of sprouts used in salads and vegetable dishes in Hawai'i. Most can be found in Asian or natural foods stores.

**Star anise:**
Brownish seeds with eight points that taste like licorice.

**Star fruit:**
A waxy, light green fruit; also called carambola. Cut in cross section, it reveals a five-pointed star shape. Trim the points off the stars if the points are too dark for your taste.

**Sticky rice:**
A glutinous short-grain white rice used in Thai cuisine. Sticky rice is steamed in baskets and is often used in Thai desserts.

**Strawberry papaya:**
A small papaya with pinkish flesh and black seeds.

**Sweet chili sauce:**
See Thai chili paste.

**Szechuan chili paste:**
A Northern Chinese spicy chili paste using chilies, garlic, oil, and salt.

# T

**Tako:**
The Japanese name for Hawaiian octopus. A popular appetizer prepared as poke or smoked.

**Takuan:**
A yellow pickled daikon radish available bottled in Japanese markets.

**Tamarind:**
A brown, bean-shaped pod from the tamarind tree. The fruit is sweet-sour, and is made into sauces, candy, and pastes.

**Tapa cloth:**
A feltlike fabric made from the pounded bark of the wauke, or mulberry, tree. Traditionally used by the Hawaiians for clothing, bedding, and canoe sails.

**Taro:**
A starchy root of the taro, called kalo, is pounded to make poi. Its flavor is similar to artichokes or chestnuts. The leaves (lū'au) and stems (hāhā) are also used in cooking. Taro contains an irritating substance and must be cooked before any part of the plant can be eaten.

**Taro leaves:**
See lū'au leaves.

**Thai basil:**
A green and red variety of basil. Substitute fresh sweet basil.

**Thai chili paste:**
A slightly sweet, thick, hot bottled paste of garlic, vinegar, and chilies. Sriracha® is a brand name.

**Thai curry paste:**
Yellow, red, and green curry pastes used in many Thai and Southeast Asian sauces. Yellow is generally the mildest and green the hottest.

**Thai ginger:**
See galangal.

**Tiger shrimp:**
A large saltwater shrimp with a striped shell.

**Tiparos® fish sauce:**
A brand of bottled Filipino fish sauce used to season many Asian dishes.

**Ti leaf:**
The leaves of the ti plant. Used to steam and bake fish and vegetables. Often called "Hawaiian aluminum foil." Substitute banana leaves, grape leaves, or even corn husks. Available at wholesale florist shops.

**Tobiko:**
The orange roe of the flying fish. Similar to caviar, it has a mild flavor and slight crunch. It is available in red, black, and green in Japanese markets.

**Tofu:**
The Japanese name for soybean curd. Available fresh in Asian markets.

**Togarashi:**
Japanese red pepper flakes, also called ichimi. Substitute red pepper flakes.

# V

**Venison:**
Island deer are hunted primarily on the islands of Lānaʻi, Molokaʻi, and Hawaiʻi. Because it has so little fat, venison is usually marinated or cooked slowly in liquid. Venison is a favorite meat for pipikaula, a version of beef jerky.

**Vietnamese chili paste:**
An extremely spicy paste of garlic, vinegar, and chilies.

# W

**Wana:**
A purple sea urchin considered a delicacy by Hawaiians and Japanese.

**Warabi:**
See fiddlehead ferns.

**Wasabi:**
The Japanese name for a root that resembles horseradish. It is most often sold in cans as powder or paste.

**Won bok:**
Cabbage-like vegetable, also called napa or Chinese cabbage.

**Wonton wrappers:**
Thin sheets of noodle dough used to wrap food for frying or steaming.

# Mail-Order Sources

**Albert Uster Imports, Inc.**
9211 Gaither Road
Gaithersburg, MD 20877
Telephone 1-800-231-8154
www.auiswiss.com

A professional source for confectionary and bakery supplies and tools, including edible gold dust.

**Aloha Shoyu Company**
96-1205 Waihona St.
Pearl City, HI 96782

Telephone (808)-456-5929
Fax (808) 456-5093
www.alohashoyu.com

A producer of specialty cooking sauces, with distributors on the West Coast. Call for information on an outlet near you.

**Aquaculture Associates, Inc.**
P.O. Box 301
Kahuku, HI 96731
Telephone 1-800-542-4459 or
    (808) 293-1230

A grower and wholesaler of Hawaiian edible seaweeds such as ogo. Call for information on a supplier in your area.

**Aquaculture Development Program**
Department of Land and Natural
    Resources
1177 Ala Kea St., #400
Honolulu, HI 96813
Telephone (808) 587-0030
Fax (808) 587-0033
www.hawaiiaquaculture.org

This department acts as a clearinghouse of information for Hawaiian aquaculture products and can put you in touch with a wholesaler or farm, as well as direct you to a store in your area. Fresh products are available mostly on the West Coast.

**D'Artagnan**
280 Wilson Ave.
Newark, NJ 07105
Telephone 1-800-327-8246
Fax 973-465-1870
www.dartagnan.com

Fresh foie gras, plus sausages, ducks and duck fat, and other specialty items.

**Fresh Island Fish**
3100 Ualena St.
Honolulu, HI 96819
Telephone (808) 831-4911
Fax (808) 836-8762
www.freshislandfish.com

A wholesaler of ocean-caught or aquacultured fresh Hawaiian fish for export to mainland restaurants and distributors. They specialize in snapper, sashimi-grade ahi, mahimahi, ono, and swordfish. They will retail directly to the consumer, but it can be expensive.

**Hana Herbs**
P.O. Box 323
Hana, HI 96713
Telephone and Fax (808) 248-7407
www.maui.net/~hanaherb/

A wholesaler of Hawaiian herbs such as lemongrass and Thai basil. Will ship by Federal Express to professional chefs and distributors.

**Hawaiian Fruit Specialties, Ltd.**
P.O. Box 637
Kalaheo, HI 96741
Telephone (808) 332-9333
Fax (808) 332-7650

This retail supplier will mail island jams, jellies, mango chutney, and syrups.

**Hawaiian Vintage Chocolate Company**
1050 Bishop St., Suite 162
Honolulu, HI 96813
Telephone 1-800-735-8494
www.hwvi.com

High-quality white, semisweet, and dark chocolate produced on the Big Island of Hawai'i. Available both wholesale and retail.

**Kitchen Crafts, Inc.**
2410 W. 79th Street
Merrillville, IN 46307

Confectionary and bakery supplies and tools.

**Langenstein Farms**
P.O. Box 615
Honaunau, HI 96726
Telephone 1-800-621-5365
Fax and message, 800-328-9891
www.kona-coffee.com/konastore/

A top-quality grower of sun-dried, air-roasted 100 percent Kona estate coffee available in several roasts. Brochure and order form available.

**MacFarms of Hawai'i**
3615 Harding Avenue, No. 207
Honolulu, HI 96816
Telephone (808) 737-0645
Fax (808) 734-4675
www.macfarms.com

Unsalted dry-roasted macadamia nuts and other macadamia products by mail.

**Mauna Loa Macadamia Nuts**
1 Macadamia Rd.,
H.C. 01, P.O. Box 3
Hilo, Hawai'i, HI 96720
Telephone (808) 966-8612
www.maunaloa.com

Macadamia nut products and Kona coffee.

**Oils of Aloha**
P.O. Box 685
Waialua, HI 96791
Telephone 1-800 367-6010 or
(808) 637-5620
Fax (808) 637-6194
www.oilsofaloha.com

Producers of macadamia nut oil. A mail-order catalogue is available.

**Orchid Isle Chèvre**
Ku'oko'a Farm
P.O. Box 452
Kurtistown, HI 96760
Telephone (808) 966-7792

Producer of high-quality goat cheese. They make fresh chèvre, chèvre in olive oil, and feta on the Big Island of Hawai'i. Mail order available.

**Penzeys Ltd**.
Merchants of Quality Spices
P.O. Box 1448
Waukesha, WI 53187
Telephone 1-800-741-7787
Fax 262-785-7678
www.penzeys.com

A wonderful source of spices and herbs by mail. A mail-order catalogue is available.

**Rooster Farms Coffee Company**
P.O. Box 471
Honaunau, HI 96726
Telephone (808) 328-9173
Fax (808) 328-9378
www.roosterfarms.com

Producer of sun-dried handpicked 100 percent Kona coffee. Both regular and organically grown coffees are available. A mail-order brochure is available.

**Sweet Celebrations**
P.O. Box 39426
Edina, MN 55439
Telephone 1-800-328-6722
Fax (612) 943-1688
www.sweetc.com

A complete catalogue of confectioners' supplies, including chocolate and other ingredients, and equipment.

**Take Home Maui, Inc.**
121 Dickenson Street
Lāhainā, HI 96761
Telephone (808) 661-8067
Fax (808) 661-1550
www.maui-activities.com

A mail-order source for Maui onions, fresh pineapple and papaya, and macadamia nut products.

**The Oriental Pantry**
423 Great Road 2A
Acton, MA 01720
Telephone (978) 264-4576
Fax (781) 275-4506
www.orientalpantry.com

An extensive and helpful mail-order source for Asian cooking utensils and foods ranging from Thai chili paste to lemongrass and hoisin sauce. Call for mail-order catalogue.

**Wilton Enterprises, Inc.**
2240 West 75th Street
Woodridge, IL 60517
Telephone 1-800-794-5866
Fax 1-888-824-9520
www.wilton.com

Pastry and cake decorating supplies, paste food colors, and icing ingredients.

# Index

to handle, 152
Hawaiian or Thai, 70, 94, 98, 136, 153
   to prepare, 152
to roast and peel, 152-153
Thai, 90, 91
   vinaigrette, 64-65
   *see also* chili(es), Hawaiian or Thai
chili oil, 142
chili paste, 81
   Chinese, 62
   Thai, 13, 64, 87
chili pepper water, 28, 39
   to make, 153
chives
   infused in oil, 7
   in salad, 22
chocolate, 142-145
   bittersweet
      in crème brûlée, 99
      in filling, 122
      for garnishing, 109, 122, 143-145
      for sauce, 142-143
   buttercream, 122
   coating (couverture), 106
   crème brûlée, 98
   discs, 122
      to make, 144
   filigree, to make, 145
   garnishes, 122
      to make, 143-145
   Hawaiian vintage, 99, 109, 114, 143
   leaves, 122-123
      lattice, to make, 144-145
   and macadamia nut cake, 106
   to melt, 143
   pie, 120
   to pipe, 143
   sauce, 142-143
   semisweet, 142
   shapes, flat, to make, 144
   to temper, 143
   tulip petals, 122-124
      striped, to make, 144-145
   unsweetened, 142-143
   white, 120, 144
   wings
      to assemble, 123
      to make, 144
      striped, to make, 144
Choy, Sam
   lū'au thrown by, 131
   recipes from, 10, 84
cilantro
   purée, 28

citrus
   and herb butter, 141
coconut
   crème fraîche, 102
      to grate, 145
   to prepare, 145
   to shell, 145
   to toast, 145
coconut milk, 84, 91, 102
   to make, 145-146
coffee
   in crème brûlée, 98-99
      leftover grounds, 98
coriander and butter sauce, 73
coriander seed, 73, 90
corn,
   baby, 58
corn cakes, 47
cornmeal, 47
coulis
   fruit, 148
   guava, 117
cream
   ginger, 55
   sour, 22
   *see also* pastry cream
cream puffs
   to make, 146
crème anglaise, 146-147
crème brûlée
   chocolate, 99
   five spoons of , 98-100
   Kona mocha, 98
   liliko'i, 98
   mango, 98
   Thai, 98
crème fraîche, 22
   coconut, 102
   to make, 103
croutons, 147
   garlic, 147
   herb, 147
   sourdough, 31
   toasted, 22
crust
   for chocolate pie, 120
cumin, 39, 90
cups
   chocolate, 123-124
curry
   sauce, 87, 91
custard
   to avert lumping, 146-147

# D

Daelemans, Kathleen, 120
daikon, 4
*see also* sprouts
demi-glacé
Beef, to make, 158-159
veal, to make, 158-159
dill, and mayonnaise sauce, 25
dressing, 22
Asian, 10-11
sesame, 67
for Thai chicken, 53
*see also* vinaigrette
duck
kālua, with plum wine sauce, 58
stock, homemade, 157-158
duck fat, 58-59
to render, 154

# E

eau-de-vie, 148-149
eggplant, 90
in 'ahi cake, 2
napoleon, 7
in terrine, 19
egg whites
in biscuit, 106
in meringue, 122
in mousse, 117
egg yolks, 106
in buttercream, 122
in crème anglaise, 146
in crème brûlée, 98, 99
in ice cream, 102, 149-150
in mousse, 117
Ellman, Mark, recipes from, 28, 55, 109
endive, curly. See frisèe
Eng, Robert, 111

# F

Ferguson-Ota, Amy, 19, 53, 67
fiddlehead (pohole)
salad, 67
filling
chocolate pie, 120
for gyoza, 64
lumpia, 13
fish
'ahi
cake, 2
charred shichimi, 4-5
nori, Keāhole, 10-11
and taro salad, 28
*see also* fish, tuna

kūmū
papillote of, 79
togarashi-seared, 67-68
mahimahi
crusted, 84-85
sautèed, 87
marlin, in poke, 10
moana, with prawns, 16-17
moonfish. *See* fish, opah
onaga
pan-seared fillet of, 90-92
'ōpakapaka
jasmine tea-steamed fillet of, 73
with sesame-chili sauce, 94
redfish, in bouillabaisse, 16
red snapper, as a substitute, 67, 79, 90
lomi lomi, 136
and shrimp gyoza, 64-65
white-fleshed, as a substitute, 16, 94
fish sauce
patic, 39
Thai (nam pla), 13
Tiparos® brand, 40, 91
fish stock, 17
to make, 157
five-spice powder, Chinese, 50
food processor, to make ice cream in, 150
frisèe (curly endive), 22
fruit
with ice cream, 109
ice cream, 150
puree, uncooked (coulis), 148
sorbet, 150
fruit juice, to make, 148
Fruitsource® (liquid sweetener), 120

# G

galangal, 87
ganache, 123
honey and Hawaiian vintage chocolate, with gold-dusted chocolate leaves
and poha berry sauce, 114-115
to make, 142
Gannon, Beverly, recipes from, 47, 62
garlic
to make, 141
and herb butter, 76, 140-141
to roast, 154
roasted, 55
garnishes, chocolate, 123, 142-145
ginger
cream, 55
crystallized, 99
in marinade, 55
pickled, 55, 87

and poha berry butter, 50
in marinade, 55
pickled, 55, 87
and poha berry butter, 50
gold leaf, 114
Goto, Edwin, 22
graham crackers, 120
green onions. *See* scallions
greens, mixed baby, 10, 53, 67
guava, coulis, 117
gyoza, shrimp and salmon, 64

# H

half-and-half, 142, 149
haricots verts, 67
hazelnut meringue, 122
herb
butter, 140, 141
salad, 22
sauce, 25
Hetzel, Mark, 102
honey
Kiawe, 114
lehua, 81

# I

ice cream
fruit, 150
green tea, 150
macadamia nut, 150
to make without a machine, 150
pineapple, 102
vanilla, 149-150
imu (baking pit), 132

# J

Johnson, David Paul, recipes from, 7, 31, 58
Josselin, Jean-Marie, 64
juice, fruit
to make, 148
to reduce, 148

# K

kaffir lime leaves, 16, 87, 90, 98
Kaleohano, Gerard, 36
kecap manis, 55
Kim, OnJin, 4, 94
kirsch, 117
kiwi fruit, 109

# L

ladyfinger, 109
lamb

chops
to "French," 147
Indonesian grilled, 55
five-spiced smoked, 50
to smoke, 51
laulau, steamed seafood, 25
lemongrass, 16, 87
in bouillabaisse, 16
in crème brûlée, 98
in curry paste, 90
in marinade, 50
in sauce, 91
lemon juice, 140-141
lettuce
butter, 36
red leaf, 36
liliko'i (passion fruit)
crème brûlée, 98
to prepare, 147
puree, 13
and soy sauce, 4
*see also* passion fruit
lime juice, 47, 64, 141
limpets. *See* shellfish, 'opihi
limu (seaweed), 39
*see also* ogo
linguiça, 62
liqueur
anise-flavored, 149
Chambord, 123
coffee-flavored, 106
crème de cassis, 149
Grand Marnier, 117
Kahluá, 106
raspberry, 123, 149
lomi lomi, 136
Longworth, Michael, 25
lū'au, traditional, 129-138
lumpia wrapper, 13

# M

macadamia nut(s), 84
and chocolate cake, 106
ice cream, 109, 150
to shell, 151
mango, 109
crème brûlée, 98
to prepare, 147
spicy sauce, 13
marinade
for chicken, 53
for lamb, 50, 51, 55
marionberries, 109
marzipan, 123